After College When You Don't Have A Plan

UNEDITED

By: Elizabeth Rochelle FeelJoy

After College When You Don't Have A Plan

Published by: Elizabeth Rochelle FeelJoy
Cover & Design: Elizabeth Rochelle FeelJoy
Copyright © 2018 Elizabeth Rochelle FeelJoy

Visit me on my Facebook page

https://www.facebook.com/After-College-When-You-Dont-Have-A-Plan-763904013806710/?view_public_for=763904013806710

For direct link sales through Amazon

http://www.amazon.com/dp/0692086609
http://www.amazon.ca/dp/0692086609

For direct link Europe sales through amazon

http://www.amazon.co.uk/dp/0692086609
http://www.amazon.de/dp/0692086609
http://www.amazon.es/dp/0692086609
http://www.amazon.fr/dp/0692086609
http://www.amazon.it/dp/0692086609

ISBN-13: 978-0692086605
ISBN-10: 0692086609

Ponder the path of thy
feet, and let all thy
ways be established.

KJV Proverbs 4:26

P.S: Now you tell me…

Contents

Chapter 1
Right after College..10

Chapter 2
New York Arrival..21

Chapter 3
Chicago...44

Chapter 4
Back to Tennessee..85

Chapter 5
State-to-state..94

Chapter 6
Back to Tennessee part 2..109

Chapter 7
New York again..128

Chapter 8
Florida..141

Chapter 9
Tennessee; bloom where you are planted...148

Chapter 10
Moral of the story..160

Dedication

I dedicate this book, whether a success or failure, to my college professor; Dr. Randall Egdorf, and my constant cheerleader over the years, Don Harris, for the publication of this book. Professor Dr. Egdorf, thank you for giving your class the assignment to write a book for a grade; by which, I would have never become interested in writing in the first place. My first book: Human Seasons, thank God it just sits in your storage boxes, filled with other student's projects from over the years. Don; even when we worked at that pizza joint together back in college, you were more excited than I was when this book was just an idea. Thanks Don, I hope I made you both proud.

RIGHT AFTER COLLEGE

Chapter 1
Right After College

When handed my diploma, a stern voice called out:

"Elizabeth Ann Payne." followed by cheers from the stance. That moment has echoed in my mind from time to time. It's ironic; in addition to living my life as an Elizabeth, the Ann guaranteed me to suffer *Payne* as well. According to House of Names; Payne is a French surname for peasant, or a person who lives in the country as opposed to urban city, and a person who's religious beliefs are suspect. I had not realized that before writing this book, that names can create major influences.

In December of 2007, I moved to Tara, Tennessee straight out of college from Springfield, Illinois. At 24 years old I obtained a Bachelor's degree in Communications. After graduation, I was not promised employment anywhere, it was more like: *Here's your degree, now go out into the world and make it.* It was not my intent to stay in Tara. I had signed myself up for housing in Springfield before I left. Housing is low-income apartments given to those on low or no income. I got approved, but the apartment I got was being rehabbed on and would take until the end of January to be ready to move into, and it was just the beginning of December. My Aunt, who was a Pastor, and pushing sixty years old, convinced me to stay with her in Tara and help out with her church instead.

Right After College

At first, it was good; getting to know all my relatives from my stepmother's side of the family. I became best friends with my cousin Valarie; who, like me, just graduated from college a year before with a Bachelor in Education. She took me to Dallas, Texas to visit her friends. By this time it was April of 2008 and the weather was turning from winter to spring. I had the best time visiting all over Dallas. When we came back to Tara, I got a job as a hostess at a small restaurant and secured another job at the fire department as a 911 emergency operator. But staying with my aunt was costly. I had gotten two phones turned on in my name for her; I was paying her tithes and offering for the church, paying to stay at her house, while paying my own bills (phone, credit cards, and school loans). At the end of the month, I had barely enough to catch the bus to go back and forth to work. Eventually I got my own apartment in July of 2008, but by that time I had already quit the hostess job and feared losing my permanent one at the fire department. I had gotten hired in April and was still training in July.

I worked above a fire station in an enclosed office with tented windows. Inside were large computer monitors, but the space itself was small. I was given a badge that read: Agent. I was excited about the idea of this job and serving my community in this way, but the job itself was tedious. I shared this small space with only older women who had been there for years. I was assigned a trainer who carried out the impossible of making a person feel both uncomfortable and comfortable at the same time. She had a matter-of-fact personality used to answer the emergency calls, only she kept it throughout the day and was never seen without it. The office, for the most part was relaxed. I had the day shift of which I was not prepared for. My body did not wake up until noon. The rules were: Be late and tardy as less as possible, know your job, and respect the privacy of your

After College When You Don't Have A Plan

callers. My trainer explained to me that in the office I will see my co-workers gossip, read a book between calls, or even watch television. But; she explained the difference between me and them was that they know their jobs, so if I chose to participate I better damn well know the job; a warning I did not heed. I was 24 years old at the time and this was my first real job. I did not have a car, so at 6a.m every morning I'll wake up and head out walking, alone, down streets, and under viaducts or bridges, to be at work by 7a.m. My body always had a mind of its own so I was often late: Strike 1. Between arguments that broke out between my trainer and her co-worker, I was not being taught anything and I was not allowed to touch the computer equipment used to do the job. I felt like I was in a no win situation, but I was told I could come onto other shifts to shadow co-workers. My body was barely making it back and forth to my shift, so to take on an extra shift for more training seemed like more work than I was willing to put in. I did it sometimes, but it left me completely exhausted; Strike 2. Sometimes in the office I would over hear co-workers gossip candidly about an emergency call they had received. One day; while I was training, the receiver that allows managers to hear what's going on in the office clicked on. I was next to that button but I swear to God I did not click it on, but some co-workers suspected I did. One-by-one I was alienated from my co-workers; Strike 3. About this time my trainer went on vacation and I was given a much older (still pretty) and much grumpier trainer. Her personality toward me was sly. I felt as though I was always being tested. She'll say things to me and record my responses to co-workers in the office. My original trainer was like that too, but less obvious about it. Two days before my birthday I let everyone know that I would be bringing my own cake to the office. Everyone seemed to look forward celebrating my 25th birthday with me. However; the day before, when I was finalizing

Right After College

the preparations, little did I know the office was prepping my departure. My trainer gave me a stack of papers to sign. When I read it, it stated that I was incompetent to the details of the job. When I asked about this she assured me that by signing it was a way to keep my job and I would be given more training, all said with a smile on her face. No sooner did I sign was I called into an office. Inside waiting for me was my witty and gay office manager, who also seemed eager to celebrate my birthday, and the department's head manager. The first sentence spoken was:

"Well; after today you won't be here anymore.", and worse yet I had to go out and face my coworkers, collect my things, and leave. It was the middle of July, right before my birthday turning 25 years old, and they let me go. Here I was: A year older, unemployed, and worse I just signed a year's lease on an apartment.

Thankfully, I got another job with a local college. It paid a couple of cents more and it was a travel position. I would have been all set, but the college was in danger of closing and after only a week I was let go from that job as well. Tara was a mid-size town, so if you are not working for the city or the college, you were out of luck job wise. As the months passed I hustled for work at retail stores and places where one works and get paid the same day called: Temporary Day Labor Services (temp service jobs). I even worked as a garbage woman for a day to make rent. The downside to these jobs was that they send out mostly men. People worked there as a last result. Some employees were homeless and didn't carry good hygiene. The day starts as early as 5 o'clock a.m., only to sit around on steel folding chairs until your name is called for an assignment. Around 9 o'clock a.m., names' being called starts to dwindle, and at some places angry outbursts, followed by threats, begins to breaks out. I stayed in Tara for a

After College When You Don't Have A Plan

year and a half and I hated it. It was 2009 and I still had not found permanent employment. I had no car and no money to catch the bus so I walked everywhere. I was so poor that I received food stamps each month just to make it by.

In 2009, the most the state would allow single individuals receiving food stamps was one hundred and sixty dollars (Wikipedia. 2017, Nov 9). Most of that went to my other Aunt, who was just a couple of years younger than Pastor Aunt. The other aunt lived close near me. In return for driving me to the grocery store, with what seemed like a million bags of groceries, I was supposed to only give her thirty dollars' worth of my food stamps, but it always seemed to be more than that. She would get food on my stamps to sell and turn into a profit at her church. This routine usually kept me starving towards the middle of the month. I did not make any friends in Tara; my only other contacts were family members and Pastor Aunt's church friends who were 50 and older.

With my Bachelor's degree the best job I could get was a house-keeping position, I started that March of 2009. Having a personal relationship in Tara was even worse. The best relationship I could get into was with a man who was older than both my parents and he didn't even live in Tara, he lived a couple of miles out in Lord, Tennessee. In the beginning I didn't want to be with him, after all he was friends with my almost sixty-year-old Pastor Aunt. A couple of nights before we happened, he showed up when I was with another guy. On the night we happened the old guy confronted me, his response was: If I can give it to that guy I could give it to him. Just as he was about to leave, he walked back up my stairs that lead into my apartment. He took my hand and led me in my room. My mind was racing with panic, but I had no reaction until that last second when I

Right After College

tried to push him away. I thought: *No! He's friends with Pastor Aunt*. But it was too late, he held down my arms and pushed through. I didn't want to say I'd been raped, after all I was Elizabeth Ann Payne, and I had a huge ego, so I pretended to enjoy it. Afterwards; he felt like any other young guy so I continued to be with him. Thanks to his family he owned his own house. He also just brought a brand new truck, took me out almost every night, and brought me flowers. Before him, I was dating this young guy I met at one of those day labor jobs; which happened to be the one the old guy caught me with. He was beautiful and I never dated someone so attractive. He too forced himself on me in the beginning. He said:

"I couldn't hang out with you that long without having slept with you." But; that didn't last long, he kept leaving and that is how I ended up with the old guy. Before both of them, I met this other guy at a bus stop, he left me twice. Once; when I lost my job at the fire department as an emergency operator, but then he came back with a bottle of wine when I got the job at the college. Then; when I lost that job too, he never came back. And before him, when I was still living with Pastor Aunt, there was the fake music artist. At one point I thought I wanted to sing and produce music straight out of college because I had written some songs. It turned out that the fake music artist had a preexisting family, and his girlfriend of many years somehow got my telephone number. It was safer for me to just end it. During him, when I went off to Dallas for a spring vacation with my cousin Valarie, there was a brief fling with one of her male friends. I was so use to being sexually satisfied with one person I dated in college, that when college ended and there was no one person there to satisfy my needs, love suddenly had many faces.

After College When You Don't Have A Plan

By the time I got with the old guy, I was settled into my apartment. It was also the end of 2008, around the holiday season where I got a temp job at Macy's. To him, I was a single, young, woman; living on my own with a job. But after we had been dating and I got laid off my seasonal job, he saw how hard I tried to maintain that image. I ended up borrowing money from him that I could not pay back. It got to the point where he only came to my place at odd hours of the night. By then my utilities had gotten cut off. He claimed he was in the same situation I was in; in-between jobs and no money, but he managed to keep his utilities on. He came over for the last time, embraced me, and then left me in my dark apartment with no air conditioning. It was May of 2009 and the weather down south was unbearably hot. I asked if I could stay over his place for the night, he told me no and left me there. Tara, TN was no longer a place for me.

In the first grade, for the second time around, I had this anorexic and mean lady as my teacher. Back then in 1991, teachers were just getting the memo about hitting their students, but my teacher kept doing it. One day she hit me on my lips with the back of her hand, wearing a ring. The students in class lied and said I mumbled something against her. My whole lips were swollen. Also; she would consistently threaten me, in front of the entire class that I would be back in the first grade for the third time around. So; on my way in from class, I saw this girl who use to be in one class but was now in another class. I asked:

"How did you get out of one class and is now in another?"

"I got transferred." she said. I went home that night and discussed it with Stepmom. Then; I too got transferred into another teacher's class and even better, was able to pass onto the second grade. From then on; when faced with a bad situation, I would *transfer* and pass onto a new situation no matter the costs.

After College

    I got a job again, this time working as a house-keeper with a Bachelor's degree and other odd jobs to save up and break Right away. It was my dream since I was sixteen-years-old to live in New York. I had visited New York three years before in college while on spring break. I figured with all the businesses there that was where all the better jobs would be. It was now June of 2009 and my family tried to talk me out of going to New York. My stepmother even called from South Chicago (a suburb of Chicago), but I had made up my mind and was going. As soon as my lease ended at the end of June, I paid for a one-way bus ticket loaded with church members from another church going on vacation to New York. Everyone on the bus assumed I was a part of the crowd and did not know my full intentions to get off the bus and find my destiny. It was not much of a plan on my part, but it beat wasting my life away in a mid-size town working as a maid with a Bachelor's degree.

After College When You Don't Have A Plan

COMMENTS

Leave a comment...

Vicky127

Omg! A house-keeper with a Bachelor's degree! Yea; might have better luck moving to a bigger city, like how you transferred out of that teacher's class that threaten to hold you back a grade again, but so far this is ridiculous, and unacceptable.

Miketheman

Vicky127 I agree. But how is this person going to live once in New York?...without a plan?

Elizabeth Rochelle FeelJoy

Vicky127 and Miketheman have you learned a lesson in this first chapter? Or had one of those *ah ha* moment yet? I encourage you to keep reading and all will reveal itself.

NEW YORK ARRIVAL

After College When You Don't Have A Plan

Chapter 2

New York Arrival

Once I arrived, just looking out over the city as the bus passed took my breath away. That Jay-Z and Alicia Keys song: *Empire State of Mind*, had not even come out yet, but the lyrics: *bright lights of New York*, did inspire me. At about three in the morning, with only two hundred dollars in my pocket, no hotel reservation, and a tired body filled with fantasies, hope, and excitement I wandered the busy dark streets of New York, unafraid. I went into a pizza restaurant trying to buy the time until morning, but I ate too quickly, so I wandered again. I saw steps that people, whom I assumed were homeless, were lying on. These were tall steps that led up to this big, brick, building which I later discovered was just an old post office on 34th street. I went up to the very top and looked down on the city that I lied, cheated, and hung up on my stepmother just to get to. The city was so beautiful, with the night light twinkling in the distance, that it made all that I had done to get there seemed worth it. There was a guy staring at me from across the enormous steps I was sitting on.

He came up to me and introduced himself as Skeet.

"I live in Jersey, but I come out here on the weekends to sober up after partying." he said. He was taller than me, a white man, thin, and looked like he was in his late twenties. We talked until daylight broke in. I shared my candy with him that was from my sack lunch on the trip up here, and he listened as I told him all my dreams and intentions in New York.

New York Arrival

"I want to get a career going, advertising commercials for businesses." I told him. *Hey, my degree is in communications, I might as well use it-* I thought. He was the first person who did not say I would fail and was easy to talk to. When day light came he pointed the way to a shelter that would feed me and where I could possibly get some sleep. But when I arrived they told me:

"We no longer take in the homeless." and I was referred to another place a little further away. When I arrived there I discovered it was a food line where they fed the homeless. I found myself in line with other homeless people, sitting on an open curb, next to a building, where people walking by could see me being called into that building where they would feed us. And still I had high hopes, I was in New York.

At this point, I had only two hundred dollars or less in my pocket and nowhere to go, but I did not consider myself homeless. I felt above them. Maybe it was because I had a college degree or because I voluntarily gave up my apartment when my lease was up instead of being evicted into homelessness. But I was completely jaded at the experience of waiting in a food line with both sane and mentally ill homeless people. I went in and exchanged my identification card for assistance. The people working there did not give us much time to eat. They wanted us in and out quickly. The workers looked at us like we were wasting up their time and talked down to us like we were abusing the system by seeking their help. But still I had high hopes because I was in New York. When we left they gave us back our identification cards. Yet, again, I was left stranded in the mid-morning with no place to go. I needed some sleep, even if it was just for an hour. I tried to think. I thought of the major's office: *They'll know of places that would take me in.* When I got there,

After College When You Don't Have A Plan

no one knew what department dealt with my situation, so they referred me to a church next door, St. Andrews'. From there I finally got the assistance I was searching for. I met with Friar Gode` and he provided me with a phone and a list of shelters. I finally got one that agreed to take me in. I would have to travel out of New York City into Brooklyn to get there, but as tired and sleepy as I was, I did not mind.

When I got to the shelter in Brooklyn, I was searched. The building itself looked like a prison. I was told that the building use to be a school a long time ago. Since then, barb wire and steel bars had been placed on the windows and around the premises. There were thick cemented steps that led up to the gruesome building and inside were metal detectors as you came through the heavy wooden double doors just in front of the building. There was another set of wood doors alongside of it, those were the exit doors. Right next to the metal detector were two huge computer monitor screens and a conveyor belt, both used to spy on people's belongings as they entered inside. Security went through my belongings and discovered I had a laptop and told me I could not bring laptops in. They would hold it up to 24 hours, but then I would have to find some place to put it. I had a mirror, disposable camera, some razors, and a pair of scissors my aunt gave me, all of which was not allowed. It was all thrown away except for my disposable camera and laptop. I did not care; I had found some place to lay my tired body. But I found that it was not as simple as just that.

When I finally passed the security check and went into the building, I was seen by an adviser after hours of sitting in the lobby. She took me into her office so she could enter me into the system. She asked:

New York Arrival

"What led you to the shelter?" I explained with great enthusiasm,

"I came to New York for better employment and a better life." She cursed me out, then got other women in the office to rally in on it too, then said to me:

"Welcome to New York!" But still my hopes were high; I might not have been in New York City, but it was only fifteen minutes away.

I was finally assigned a bed, A76, and I slept from that mid-afternoon until the next morning. When I awoke, I ate breakfast and sat out in the lobby for another couple of hours waiting to see a case manager. Her name was Ms. Smith; she too cursed me out once she heard my story. She was no help at all. Ms. Smith did not assign me to places that could lead me to a job, she did not arrange for me to get welfare assistance such as food stamps, cash assistance, or a Medicaid card, and she did not try to get me a clothing voucher so I could get clothes. In fact, the only thing she did do was send me upstairs to the second floor for my medical evaluation such as a T.B shot and psychological assessment so that Ms. Smith can get paid. After completing all of that I got my laptop from security and went out into the neighborhood searching for a place I could put it while I was in the shelter. I discovered I was in, what politics would call, an industrial neighborhood. These were the kinds of businesses that stayed far away from rural neighborhoods because their business created toxic fumes and waste. So, how convenient that the shelter was right next door to it. I would wake up every morning to the stink of meat being slaughtered, or a steel mining business grinding its fumes in the air. It was not fair, but at least I was not sleeping out in the elements of it. After hours of wandering the streets and thinking of places to put my laptop, I walked into a

After College When You Don't Have A Plan

place that sold storage's and put it there. It cost me fifty dollars for just half of the month that was left but I was desperate and needed to check back in at the shelter. I had to be in by 10p.m., I did not know what would happen if I came in late, but I did not want to find out either, so I came in. Still having to go through security check, every day, when entering the building I survived day after day with God's help.

It was now July of 2009 and my time was up on my storage payment. I ran out of money paying for a twenty-seven dollar, seven day, Metro pass to get around the city. I paid for food also, and my birthday came, I turned 26 years old, so a present for myself too. I needed to put my laptop some place where I did not have to pay. I thought of the church, St. Andrew, that referred me to the shelter, but time was not on my side and I needed a place near me. There was a woman named Sorita that I had become friends with since being in the shelter. She was part Latino and black, medium height, with dark long curly hair. The look of her and the way she dressed suggested she was in in her mid-thirties, but she mention she just turned fifty. She smoked like a chimney and cursed a lot, but she managed to be nice to me. She suggested that I put my laptop at her sister's place, but she was not available, so she suggested her sister's downstairs neighbor, Ms. Lula. Ms. Lula and Sorita's sister lived in the Brooklyn projects, but like I said, I was pressed for time and broke.

When Sorita and I arrived at Ms. Lula's, everyone seemed friendly and nice. All were assuring me that my laptop would be safe there. I even stayed over for a few hours joking and laughing over good times. Besides; it was only going to be for one day until Sunday, then I was going to have it stored in St. Andrew's church.

New York Arrival

When I saw Sorita that night outside the shelter, just minutes before curfew, cursing out someone over the phone, she turned to me with a nervous look on her face. She told me I needed to talk to Ms. Lula. I did not even think of my laptop for some reason, I thought that someone might have gotten hurt or something. Ms. Lula is a sixty or so year old woman who, from what I gathered from my last conversation with her and her family, cooks for everyone. It was another reason I assumed I could trust something as valuable as my laptop with her. I kept asking Sorita what happened, but she told me she did not know and that I needed to talk to Ms. Lula. So, I called Ms. Lula, she started saying the same thing but that I had to talk to Sorita. This is when I started worrying about the laptop. I asked Ms. Lula:

"Is it my laptop?"

"Yes."

"Is it stolen, broken?"

"Yes."

"Which one is it?" she said:

"Stolen." My laptop was the only thing stolen in her apartment with no signs of a break-in. Ms. Lula did not report it stolen to the police, and because she lived in the projects, with no job, and in her old age, I knew she could not replace it.

When I saw Sorita and Ms. Lula in person they both reassured me they would have it replaced. I should have gotten it in writing. I even got the police involved, but one of the officers laughed in my face. The officers told me in front of Sorita and Ms. Lula and whoever else was sitting in Ms. Lula's living room, that because I voluntarily gave it to her to hold for whatever the time being, and because it was not a break-in robbery, the only

After College When You Don't Have A Plan

thing I could do was take Ms. Lula to claims court and sue. Suing someone takes a long time. After that day, I went back to Ms. Lula's apartment hoping they found my computer, but the answer was always the same:

"Come back I'm going to get you another one." until I came back that last time. Ms. Lula's whole attitude changed. She started claiming she never got to see the computer that I left there. Then she said the computer did not work, which led me to believe that she not only knew where my laptop was but she might have had a hand in stealing it too.

After that I went off! I cursed that little old lady out. I was no longer the nice girl from Tennessee; I demanded that she give me back my laptop. But her three nephews were there to defend her. They got in my face, started cursing me out, and one of them even started taking off his belt like he was going to attack me. This was the opposite experience I had when I first arrived and I was promised my laptop would be safe. Now Ms. Lula claimed: *If it was that important to you, you should not have left it here.* It was hard but I walked away like that computer meant nothing to me, like I did not have my whole life on that laptop, like I did not have files, pictures, or a book I had written: Human Seasons, that could not be replaced. I just walked back to the shelter in tears and never went back. There was nothing I could do. My laptop was gone and I would never get it back.

Meanwhile, back at the shelter, a girl's I pod came up missing, or so she said. She went into just about everyone's room, (there were about seven rooms on just one side of my two-sided floor with ten women to a room) and turned over each person's lockers. These lockers weighed tons. The girl could not have been more than a hundred pounds and at 5'4 inches tall (a little person). I guess when a person is that angry they can do

New York Arrival

extraordinary things. She yelled and threatened to slice everyone's throats in their sleep if her stuff did not come up. Security took her downstairs, only to send her right back in the same room, the same bed, and amongst the same women whom she'd threaten to kill. I could not believe it. But the rule is that the shelter cannot put you out into the streets. They can transfer you to another shelter if they have room, but they would have to keep you if otherwise.

During college; I had at least two different roommates each semester, so I was accustom to living with strangers, although nothing has quite prepared me for this situation. True; it got catty during those dorm room days. One roommate gave me the silent treatment when we weren't getting along. Another put her finger in my face, and spit on me while she yelled. But no one has threatened to slice my throat in my sleep before, now that was a new one.

She was back, but this time she got sick in the middle of the night. She started throwing up and then passed out on the floor. My bed was next to hers. I went over to her and she was on the floor next to all that she had vomited. I ran out into the hall and saw a guy from security. He was big and looked like he use to play football. I told him that there was a girl in my room passed out on the floor in her vomit. He told me he had to go do locker check. Locker check at the shelter in Brooklyn, was taking personal belongings out of the lockers they assigned to us women when they give us a bed. If we miss the 10p.m. curfew, staff would throw our belongings in a plastic bag, and then throw those bags, with our belongings inside, down four flights of stairs. He had rather do that then assist the girl who passed out on the floor in her own vomit. I just looked at him like he was the lowest of the low.

After College When You Don't Have A Plan

"Are you serious?" I asked him. He turned from me and looked in the other direction as though I was no longer standing there. After some other girls from my room came together and complained, security personnel from the shelter started coming from out of nowhere to assist the girl who had been passed out on the floor.

Since Sorita, and my horrifying experience with staff at the shelter, I did manage to make some friends and learn about some of the women staying there, like, Lauren. Like me, Lauren had her Bachelor's degree. Her major was in mathematics. She was 43 and a fire at her apartment complex took away everything she had. I no longer felt above the homeless, it had finally sunk in that I was one of them. There had been women there with jobs, cars, name brand clothing even; that lived in the shelter. A case worker told me that she is working with a fellow employee who works for the city of New York and is, like me, living in a shelter. Here I was; no job, no car, in a city where I knew no one, and for some reason I felt above the homeless because I had my Bachelor's degree.

My stuff was later thrown down four flights of stairs because I missed curfew to take myself to the hospital, but the good news was that it switched my case manager. I no longer had no caring, just there-to-collect-a-paycheck Ms. Smith. Now I met with a cynical Ms. Rowe. She had a frightening side to her, like Jackal and Hide, but she was the first case manager I had that did not use foul language with me. Ms. Rowe got me into the Back to Work (BTW) program at Back to work Incorporated. She sent me out to sign up for cash, food, and medical assistance, and she gave me a clothing voucher. After that, things were moving along. I had some place to go during the day that could lead me in the right direction on getting a job instead of roaming the

New York Arrival

unfamiliar streets of New York on my own. I was given a free weekly metro pass every week to ride the bus or train, which helped a lot on getting from point A to point B. For the first time I was given a medical card I did not have to pay for. Being poor seemed to have its benefits.

When I went to the BTW program each week, I learned some useful information, such as my rights while being in the shelter, things I was entitled to, and who I could complain to if I was not being treated fairly. At the end of the day, those all sounded well and good, as if it is what people are supposed to do. But I felt that nothing was going to change because no one cared. I was homeless, broke, and, as far as the other side cared, was just another person taking tax money from a hard-earned pay check. I was given a weekly Metro card every week for free, all my clothes shoes and personal items were given to me, and I had a bed to sleep on every night that I did not have to pay for, free use of hot showers at the shelter, and free meals three times a day. So what if I was being verbally abused by staff every time I went back into the shelter? So what if I could not eat that nasty food they served the homeless when my only other option was to starve? So what that they had men working at the shelter that were allowed to roam anywhere as long as they voiced: *Man On,* And so what that, no matter how much I asked for just an extra fan in the room where me and nine other women were, on the fourth floor, suffering in the August heat, that the member from the director's board, Mr. Auston, and a member from head security, Mr. Davis, would sit downstairs in front of an air condition and tell me they would continue to send maintenance an email at two o' clock in the morning alerting maintenance attention to the problem? A girl even passed out from the heat in those fourth floor rooms. Still; the directors did nothing about the problem, just called an ambulance for the girl and called it a day,

After College When You Don't Have A Plan

so who cares? The homeless are getting things handed to them through the generosity of tax-payer's money, staff working with- and abusing-the homeless are getting a pay check, and we are one less problem that tax-paying citizens would have to see or hear about.

Back to work, BTW program was a place to get useful information. That is how I also heard about a dentist office that either gave out free phones with minutes on it or cash for your visit. I went in for the free phone and to get my teeth cleaned. When I arrived at the dentist's office, I was told by their recruiters that they just gave out money, ten dollars for every visit. After my cleaning the receptionist handed me and the other patience's the money in a sneaky way; under the table like, as though it was an illegal act. I asked her what was it for and she claimed it was *transportation money*. The dentist told me I had cavities and to come back for some fillings. I thought that this was great; to come back to the dentist's office and get paid again!

A week later, I went back and I brought my friend Lauren with me. I did not know what to expect when I came back to get my teeth filled. I was 26 and had only been to the dentist once in my life, and that was during college for a cleaning. The Dentist gave me a couple of shots with a needle in my mouth to numb my gums, but it only numbed my lips. He drilled a hole in four of my teeth and put the fillings in. He said:

"All finished." So, I collected my *transportation money* and waited for my friend Lauren out in their lobby. My lips were so numb I could not move them to talk. I had to write words down. Spit and drool was everywhere, I needed napkins pressed against my mouth. I could not close my teeth together. The Dentist advised me not to eat until after an hour and forty-five minutes. I did not allow myself to eat until 10a.m. the next

New York Arrival

morning. My last meal before I went into the Dentist was around nine that morning before I received the fillings. I had a headache for days and my mouth was in so much pain that I got a bed pass from the shelter to sleep all that day until the next morning.

When I finally ate at 10a.m. the next day my teeth were in such agony, I panicked. I did not know what to do; first my laptop and now my teeth. I could not even close them together. I was afraid and too angry to go back to that Dentist office, so I went to another dentist. The new dentist explained that my fillings were too high, so she drilled them down for me. Also she found another set of cavities next to the fillings. I am not a dentist, but I believed my original dentist, who put the fillings in, drilled a whole in the wrong spot, missing the cavities completely and put fillings where they were not needed. The headaches, the new dentist explained, were due to white filling placed in my mouth instead of silver. The white filling has side effects that take weeks to wear off. Then, to make matters worse, the new dentist tells me:

"You cannot use that Medicaid card here to pay for the bill because during the first six months Medicaid will not pay for more than one dentist office." As poor as I was I had to pay out of my own pocket, using the last of my *transportation money*, and was stuck for six months with a dentist who messed up my teeth and my dentist experience.

Later that day, I mustered up the courage to go back to that dentist office. The dentist I had to pay for out of my pocket did not file the fillings down low enough, and because I did not pay the entire bill, I was too ashamed to ask her to work on my mouth again. So here I was, back at my original dentist's office. I sat in the lobby and as I waited I saw the receptionist give one of the recruiters (The gang of guys who stands by the door's

After College When You Don't Have A Plan

entrance and invites passerby's in to draw more business to the dentist office) a black bag. The recruiter opened it and took out little packages with marijuana inside and started selling it out in the open lobby of the dentist office. I was shocked. No one; myself included, said a word. After seeing that, I still went in the back where the dentist was when my name got called. I allowed that same dentist, who messed up my teeth, to file down the fillings he'd put in. After he'd finished he yelled at me, like I had lied just to come back for the free money. I told the receptionist that I did not even know my dentist's name. Her response:

"You don't need to know." I was not given any documents (pictures of dental x-rays or a copy of my bill), not even a pamphlet to show I had been to that dentist's office. The only thing that was done was taking my Medicaid card and swiping it through the machine so that I would be billed.

New York; the city that I lied, cheated, and hung up on my stepmother just to get to, seemed less and less worth it. I needed to get out of the shelter, I needed a job, but even that seemed impossible. The minimum wage in New York State was $7.25 per hour. The lowest rent in what people would consider the lower barrows of New York (Brooklyn, The Bronx, and etc.) was five hundred dollars and up for just a room without a kitchen, refrigerator, and stove, so basically; just renting a room. I got fed up one day. I do not know if it was the mid-August weather or what, but I went to the Mayor's office, Community Comptrollers, and whomever else I could complain to. I was not allowed to speak to the mayor directly, but I was allowed to hand in my complaints in writing and have it sent to him. In my letter to Mayor Bloomberg, I not only complained but came up with solutions about the outrageous rents that were continuously increasing. I reminded him that those who are paying rent are not

New York Arrival

paying for libraries, parks, or things within their communities because they are just renters' not home owners paying property taxes that pay for those luxuries. The money that is being paid towards renting goes directly into the landlord's pockets. It made no sense to me that rent was allowed to go up as high as it did when none of that money is being contributed to the city renters live in; and we were in a recession too! I suggested that rent be based on the value of the property, sort of like the blue book value of a car. And, in return for the cooperation of the landlords, the city of New York would pay for rehabbing their properties. It almost sounded like a child-like solution to a grown-up problem. But at least I was giving solutions not just complaints.

A day later I got an email saying that my letter had been forwarded. I went back to the shelter with a different attitude, an attitude like I was going to make it after all and that things could possibly change. All this hope with no real action, only just my concerns forwarded to different departments. Then; my only pair of flip flops broke apart in the middle of crossing the street of City Hall, and I did not have money to replace them. My shelter was far away, but the Back to work (BTW) program was nearby. BTW also gave vouchers for clothes and had a list of places to get them. After dragging my foot in my broken sandals across City Hall, into a train station, then up numerous stairs to cross more streets (walking like I was disabled), finally I reached BTW only to be given tape to bandage my sandals. I was told that most clothing places that they send clients to do not give out shoes just clothes. I bandage up my sandals and went as far to my shelter as I could without it breaking. My sandals came a loose three blocks before I got there.

Again, I dragged my foot in my broken sandals until I arrived at the shelter. I took them off and had to walk barefooted

After College When You Don't Have A Plan

on dirty concrete floors that I once saw a grown lady pee on before arriving at a toilet in the restroom. Once I got to the second floor where the clothes and shoes were, I had to wait, until finally I was told by Ms. Neal, the director over recreation and giving away clothing, to come back with a voucher (a pass given to the homeless by our case manager to get items we needed). It was approaching 5p.m. That is the time when the homeless women are allowed back in the rooms. So; I went back to my room and put on a close-toed dress shoe with a low heel that were too tight for my feet. That next day it rained and my closed-toe shoes got completely soaked in the rain. Once again, I arrived back at the shelter bare-footed on those nasty concrete floors. But I did not go to the second floor this time; I stayed downstairs to ask for a clothing voucher to get a pair of shoes. My case manager, Ms. Rowe, was off that day. I would have to get the voucher from a director, but most had gone home already. So I was seen by another case manager. This case manager told me that I would have to come back for a voucher on Monday and it was Friday. So I quickly reminded her that those clothes and shoes were voluntarily given to go towards people in need. Her response was:

"So what, I'm supposed to give you some shoes because yours is wet?" I looked at her, said the words:

"Ok", like waving up a white flag, then turned my head, and walked back upstairs to my room on the fourth floor, in silence, in shock.

Just when I thought I heard it all, New York managed to surprise me again. When the shock wore off I called the police and explained that I was just told by a case manager, who is supposed to be working to help the homeless in our time of need, that I could not have, so much, as shoes to cover my feet from donations giving to us anyway.

New York Arrival

"Is this illegal?" I was then transferred to New York's 311 systems, but, because I used up the minutes on my government-issued free cell phone, and, because it was not an emergency number, I was cut off. Enough was enough. The mayor issued a back home program for the homeless in New York. The program paid for a plane ticket out of New York to any place in the world as long as there was someone there to accept you. I asked my case manager Ms. Rowe to send me to Chicago, Illinois were my stepmother was. My stepmother had been calling me non-stop from a pay phone in the shelter anyways, begging me to come live with her.

The wait for the ticket took longer than I expected. Instead of three to five days it took two weeks. At one point they forgot to put in the request. My case manager, Ms. Rowe, had to reprocess it. During that time, I got offered a job at Opinion Access, a calling center that gives surveys over the phone. It paid seven dollars and twenty-five cents per hour but once I got confirmation that I would be going to Chicago I turned the position down.

I also used my medical card again before I left to find out important information about personal problems that I was developing. There was a free medical office inside the women's shelter I went to often. I was not diagnosed properly and the medical staff did not seem to care. So; when I got a medical card I used it at a medical clinic outside my shelter. I'm not sure if it was the braided pigtails I wore on my head or if I reminded the doctor of one of her own children, but she went the extra mile on my behalf. She and a team of doctors told me that I am (HPV) Human Papillomavirus positive and that I had (Trich) Trichomoniasis, both are (STD's) Sexually Transmitted Disease. The Trich is curable with a 7 day supply of pills but the HPV is

After College When You Don't Have A Plan

an untreatable virus; hoped to go away on its own after a few years. Another doctor explained that HPV is a common virus among young, sexually active, men and women, and that the risk are higher if you have more than one sexual partner at a time. The virus can be passed along from person to person from someone carrying HPV. Usually, there are no symptoms with HPV, but since I had Trich along with it too, it cause symptoms of itchiness and burning, which lead me to the doctor. Although there are no symptoms usually with HPV; it does however, causes visible and invisible genital warts. The doctor calls this *low risk* (risk of a cancer) HPV. *High risk* is when doctors find abnormal cells on a women's cervix. Those abnormal cells turn into cancer cells that can kill you. I was diagnosed as high risk. I had not had sex since I left Tennessee but I was sexually active before I left. The doctors told me I was lucky because they caught it early enough to just see abnormal cells instead of cancer ones.

"It could have been worse." the doctor told me. I didn't feel lucky, I felt dirty and low. I called the last person I was sexually active with, told him the circumstances, and to get himself tested. In Tennessee, I went to six different doctors without a medical card; some of those places were low income public practices and most were the emergency room. They all told me the same thing that my symptoms were just a yeast infection. New York and California in 2009 were the only two states that gave single individuals on little or no income free medical cards, which includes free prescriptions. As for my situation, I was told there was nothing that could be done from preventing the cells from progressing into cancer cells, except monitoring it and hoping for the best. I was 26 years old.

As usual, I went back to the shelter before 10p.m. and, as usual, security would go into the rooms after 11p.m. to clean out

New York Arrival

the lockers of those women who did not make it in on time. Security came into my room one evening to clean out a locker vertically from my cubical. My cubical was right by the door where people walking by; including men, could see me sleep, undress, or anything. It was always hot in my room so the women in the rooms demanded that the door stayed open. I had the idea to put a sheet over my cubical so that I could have some privacy. A few of the staff complained and probably thought that I did not deserve that option because I was just another homeless bum, but the director over the shelter allowed it. So; when head security, Ms. Ford, came in with her staff to clean out the locker vertically from mine, a member from her staff, Mr. Leon Barron, (Whom I later discovered was the same guy who refused to assist the girl who passed out in her own vomit), had purposely stood over my cubical looking at me while I was laying down trying to sleep. The sheet was around the sides of my cubical so that people walking past the door could not see me, but Mr. Barron decided he wanted to teach me a lesson. He leaned over into my cubical, pretending to write something down, while watching me lay in my bed. When I asked him to move, he replied:

"Ain't nobody looking at you." As if the dignity of the women in these shelters were not robbed enough, he had to insult me by implying that I was not worthy to be looked at by anyone. Then, to justify his actions he reminds me that Ms. Ford did ask if all ladies were decent. In the end result, Ms. Ford, who came in with him, had to tell him to move over to where the locker check was actually being performed.

After Ms. Ford and her staff left the room I felt violated. Here I was in just a t-shirt that came to my thighs, being looked at by a staff member who was supposed to protect the women at the shelter. Instead, I was being sexually harassed by one. Sure:

After College When You Don't Have A Plan

"Man on." was voiced before they came in and Ms. Ford did yell:

"Is all ladies decent?" before she and her team came in. But the locker that was being cleaned out was on the opposite end from me. There was no reason for him to stand over my cubical, just looking at me, pretending to write something down. Mr. Barron could have stood by his teammates. The next day I put in a complaint against what happened to me. Security and staff working there seemed to protect him, claiming they did not know him and they refused to give me the proper forms to lodge a complaint. So, I went as far as City Hall to log a complaint with the city's Community Comptrollers.

They sent me back to the shelter and told me that I needed more information on him, and at the time I did not even know Mr. Leon Barron's name. When I went back to get his name, the workers did not wear name badges, so, when he walked by, I casually asked a member from staff for his name and they told me. Then I guilt security into giving me the right complaint forms instead of a blank piece of paper and they gave it to me. My communications degree was finally helping me towards something. In the complaint; I put in that I was sexually harassed by Mr. Barron. Later that day Ms. Ford called me down to talk about my written complaint, she told me that sexual harassment is touching or something verbal. As a woman I could not believe this was coming from another woman. Then she asked me if I had informed my case manager Ms. Rowe about the situation and I told her I had.

Ms. Ford informed me that she would forwarded my complaint to the directors; head management over the workers in the shelter. The next day it was time for me to leave for Chicago, by this time it was the end of August of 2009. I spotted one of the

New York Arrival

directors in the lobby. Her name was Ms. Crite; she was over all the directors and staff at the shelter. I asked if she had been informed about the situation that happened to me, and she said she had not. After that, I was off to Chicago. I do not know if my complaint got taken seriously or not, but I know that I had been rushed to leave the shelter and expected never to come back.

COMMENTS

Leave a comment...

BigPaul

I don't care how many roommates I had in college, I can't imagine anything preparing a person for that sh*!%.

After College When You Don't Have A Plan

Miketheman

Did I not just say *where is this person going to stay* from the very beginning?

    Vicky127

    Miketheman Yep, you did.

    Lacy Hamilton

    Miketheman It seems like things got so out of control that moving to a bigger city seemed like the more rational choice at the time.

New York Arrival

John1294

Lacy Hamilton The grass is never greener on the other side. To go through all that, only to go live with her Stepmom? And what happens if this plan fails?

Elizabeth Rochelle FeelJoy

To everyone, are you learning some valuable lessons? Continue reading for the answers you seek.

CHICAGO

After College When You Don't Have A Plan

Chapter 3

Chicago

When I arrived at the O'Hare Airport no one was there to pick me up. Stepmom complained before I came that the airport was too far and confusing to get to but at the last minute she said she would be there. I borrowed stranger's phones (because I used all the minutes up on my phone) to check where she was and she told me she could not make it but that I should call Stepdad and ask if he could pick me up from the airport. This was already turning into a rough start. I had to use a stranger's phone again to call him and he told me he had just gotten off from work and that he was tired. He also told me he got a message from my sister, Samantha, telling him that I was at the airport and to *Pick me up*. Stepmom and Stepdad are divorced and my stepparents have a habit of purposely doing things to upset one another like telling my sister (because Stepmom refuses to talk to him) to tell Stepdad to pick me up from the airport, that is hours away, at the last minute, disregarding the fact that he may or may not have had something going on, all after she had promised to pick me up herself. I sat at that airport from three that afternoon until 9p.m. with nothing on my stomach since breakfast.

When Stepdad arrived to pick me up, it was total silence in the van. Samantha; who is 3 years younger than me, had told me before my arrival that she asked our stepfather for money to buy food. She lived by herself and worked odd jobs to make ends meet, but sometimes she came up short. His response to my sister

Chicago

was to collect cans. I was furious. So; when he met up with me at the airport and I got into his van I was not talking to him and he was not talking to me. He dropped me off at a church I used to go to when I was little. Stepmom promised this time she would pick me up from there. We said our goodbyes and I have not physically seen him since. I am the oldest out of eight and counting. Most of us knew at an early age that we could not count on our Stepparents for financial support just as though they could not count on their parents.

An hour later Stepmom arrived with my sister at the church to take me to her house. I was looking forward to a long, hot bath; I had not had one since I left Tennessee. At the shelters, they only had showers. Before I came, Stepmom assured me that everything would be fine. I had my doubts. I had explained to her before-hand that I would be coming to her with nothing. I had no job and did not know when one would become available. It was a struggle in New York to get a job. I had put in applications everywhere. I had been living in New York for over a month and had not gotten as much as a call back. I was worried that I may be a financial burden on Stepmom. That was one of the reasons that I did not immediately jump on a bus, train, or plane, and live with her. She already had my younger brothers and sisters at home that she was supporting by herself, but she told me not to worry.

She said she had a job; but failed to tell me she lost it, money coming in from going to school; but did not tell me she already spent it, and plenty of food stamps; but did not mention that it still was not enough at the end of the month because she feed my four, hungry, teenage, brothers and sisters. Before I arrived, she also did not tell me that the hot water was cut off, and because there was no gas in the house the stove did not work either. I was disappointed, but my persistent stepmother used

After College When You Don't Have A Plan

what she still had on, which was the water and the electricity, and made do. To wash up we heated water with the microwave, and to cook food she brought an electric cooking pan. I guess she waited to tell me all of this so that I would come home and be out of the shelter. In her own way she was kind. During the first couple of days, adjusting to the new system of things at Stepmom's house, I let myself rest from all I had been through. Stepmom was kind enough to give me my own room. I had a bed now instead of the cot that I slept on at the shelter. She also brought me a miniature-sized dresser to put my clothes in.

Things were looking up. After I had rested I was eager to start work so I went out looking every day. Months went by and I still had not landed a job. It was now October of 2009, and at that point Stepmom and I were not on good terms. She was not letting me use her car to look for work anymore so I mostly relied on the internet for my job searches. And after a while that privilege got taken away as well so I walked many blocks back and forth to the library every day to use the internet. My stepmother lived in the south suburbs of Chicago. The bus did not run as often as New York bus transit systems ran, and there were no subway trains out in the suburbs. I was not given a free bus pass to get around like I was in New York; here you either had to be mentally or physically disabled to qualify. I might have been out of the shelter but I miss all its free benefits.

I felt stuck; it had now been three months and I still had not found a job. It was November and the weather was getting cold. I had no money, and I could not get around except for walking distance. The businesses in my neighborhood were mostly family-owned, other business were fast food restaurants that were crowded with workers as it was. The applications I put in over the internet were being rejected, saying I was over

Chicago

qualified in education and under-qualified in experience. Stepmom and I were at each other's throats by now. At one point she said she did not want me there anymore and that I should go live with Stepdad. At least in New York the shelters could not just throw you out. The longer I stayed, the intensity got worse. One night out of the blue Stepmom called different family members asking them to take me in. Most of them lived out of state. She claimed I was not trying hard enough to find a job. She also claimed I was crazy and unbearable to live with, and thought I was a lesbian. When I did have privileges to the computer, I would look up medical findings about the HPV I had and some sites would show detailed images of private parts with the virus on them. There were other instances where we both would criticize each other's mistakes we made in the past. She would bring up that I am not married or not standing on my own two feet financially, then I would criticize her of her failed marriages and how poorly she manages my brothers and sisters living with her. It would get to the point where we were screaming at each other and then the kids would come in and start getting into it with me because I am yelling at our stepmother. The last straw, sort of speak, happened when I was in the bathroom and I overheard Stepmom, in her room, next to the bathroom, on the phone, telling god-knows-who that I had been in the shelter. She told them that I had no job and I went out at all hours of the night. This was only to go to the emergency room because my symptoms from Trich or the HPV were acting up. True; I didn't tell her where I was going, but it was an embarrassing situation that I did not want to upset her with. After hearing her phone conversation I got angry, stormed in her room, and yelled:

"I did not come all the way over here from New York for this!" she yelled back:

After College When You Don't Have A Plan

"Shut up, and mind your business.", and then threw a house-shoe at me. I picked up that house-shoe and through it back at her and then walked quickly back to the bathroom. Next thing I knew, she comes out of her room on one of her canes (she had just recently suffered a leg injury at my other sister, Beatrice's, wedding) holding the shoe in her hand and yells:

"I want you out!"

"I ain't going nowhere." I said to Stepmom. We both had signed an agreement saying that she would allow me to stay at her house for up to several months until I can get on my feet. It was taken to the currency exchange, where she paid money for it to be stamped and notarized. At this point it did not make a difference because little did I understand that if I had no lease there I had to go if she did not want me there.

There was no one I could turn to either; my stepfather was living with someone himself. Stepdad's mother was also in Chicago, but she lived with the man she worked for. She was an in-home-care giver. Even if it were possible that I could stay with her, she did not like me anyway at that time. She thought that I did not show my stepfather the respect he deserved. Meanwhile; I thought just being next to him in a car without exploding on him for being absent from my life, and only seeing him once every five years (if I am lucky), was plenty of respect. Also; at this point, I was thinking of going back to Texas where my cousin Valarie and her friends lived. I had a three hundred dollar voucher to use toward any future flight travel because the airlines messed up my flight that was scheduled to come to Chicago at a certain time. Besides, Texas was where I last remembered having so much fun, but I could not go down there without a job or else I'll be kicked out of another house within a week. My cousin and our friends were barely making it as it was. I could not go back to

Chicago

Tennessee either, there was no one to stay with except Pastor Aunt, who now had my second cousin from Mississippi, I once baby sat, living with her. I had two sisters living in Chicago. The one sister, Beatrice, who was a year younger than me, was newly married. We did not get along at all because of a disagreement we had years ago over her; then boyfriend, now husband, who use to be my friend.

It all started senior year in high school. When I failed the first grade, that permanently placed me in the same grade with my younger sister. We were at our lockers when she told me about this guy who sat in the back of her class and had conversations with himself. I liked weirdos like that. I gravitated towards him like a moth to a flame. Unfortunately; it turned out he was completely normal and just amused himself in class. Before finding this out I had already asked him to Home Coming. Somewhere along the way I got bored with him and asked another guy out and went with him instead. I thought nothing of his feelings or what kind of position that put him in, but he did. He went after my sister, and after everything I confided in her about him, she accepted his advancements and later married him while I remained single. Then Beatrice and I went to college together. I was a part of a group that I was not getting along with. So; when I left that group, they sought out Beatrice, and true to form she obliged. They became the "it" group of college and I, my sister's embarrassment. Also, I was suspicious of her over identity theft; of which, I still say to this day she had something to do with.

The other sister, Samantha, who was with Stepmom when she picked me up from the church I use to go to when I was little, lived in just a room at the YMCA. And I could not possibly go back to New York because of the sexual harassment situation.

After College When You Don't Have A Plan

Before I decided to leave New York to stay with Stepmom, she would call me on the pay phone every day. She said my dignity would be taken away if I was to stay in New York and suffer their abuse, but it was being taken away from me here, suffering her abuse. I took the little dignity I had left, packed my things, and left.

I was homeless again.

I wandered the streets from 12a.m. to about eight in the morning. It was cold and now November of 2009, the ending of fall and just the beginning of winter. I went anywhere I could find warmth. There seemed to be nobody out except me and men looking for people like me. I even went to the police station, told them my story, hoping for a warm shelter for the night. But this was not New York. They told me that the shelters do not accept people in after a certain time. I later discovered that they did if you are escorted by police. The police told me that there was nothing they could do, they let me walk out of their lobby knowing I had no place to go. I walked up and down the cold streets carrying a backpack. I saw police cars just drive past me, not caring where I would end up. I went into the emergency side of a hospital to keep warm, but the hospital was so small that people are noticed right away when they come in. In South Chicago, the hospital's policy prohibited the homeless to sit in their lobbies overnight. Things got so desperate that I went inside of a bank. The bank itself was closed, but there was a small ATM lobby located inside the front entrance that was open and warm inside. It was a twenty-four hour ATM. There I was, for hours pretending to write things down just so I could keep warm. I just stood at a desk used to write or calculate your check books.

When daylight came, I went searching for a shelter. Turns out there was something called The Day Site down the street and

Chicago

around the corner from where Stepmom lived. It was called the day site because the homeless do everything but sleep there. It was different from New York, there were not any metal detectors, but the wait time to see a staff person was pretty much the same. Once I got in, I was quickly introduced to their rules and policies. I arrived at the end of a weekday. It was not explained however, that I would have to find my own way to keep warm during the day on the weekends until 7p.m. Other people in this program who were homeless went to stay with a relative during those times, some hung out at the library, and others rented a hotel. There was no one building where the homeless resided that was open seven days a week and open all day like it was in New York. Here, it was more like five days a week until 6p.m. on most days except major holidays. Also, unlike New York shelters, where I slept in the same building, we slept at different churches in the community night after night. Some were within walking distance and some required transportation that was available three days out of the week. On other nights we would have to make it on our own to the long distant churches.

Lucky for me I had gotten a job right before Stepmom told me to leave. I had gotten hired at a grocery store in the neighborhood as a cashier. When I worked, I gave it my all, never letting on to my current situation. On the first weekend in the program, I had no place to go but I had just gotten paid. I was in a taxi on my way to a hotel when the cab driver struck up a conversation with me and offered me a proposition. He worked late nights on the weekends and said if I were to pay him I could stay at his place for the weekends. The price was reasonable, and I did not want to overpay for a hotel so I took his offer. When he dropped me off at his place the both of us were nervous. He expressed he had never let a complete stranger stay at his home

After College When You Don't Have A Plan

and I had never agreed to stay at a complete strangers home. But he trusted me and I trusted him.

There I was alone in his home. It was clean, warm, and cozy. I took a bath. I was excited because for the first time since I left Tennessee I took my first hot bath instead of showers. I felt so good that I went right to sleep. I woke up the next morning feeling great. I was in one room and he was in another. Things were going great for the low price of seventy dollars for just the weekend until he offered another proposition I had to refuse. He said that he did not want my money anymore, he wanted me instead. The guy was so much older than me, in fact; around the same age of the old guy I left in Tennessee. I had been-there-done-that dating an older guy, I was not about to make that same mistake, especially for a place to lay my head. I told him no and never spent a night at his place again. My dignity shot up about five points. I was proud of myself. As for the weekends, I spent the daytime at the library and when it was time to go to a church and sleep I took the bus or walked there.

Many times my job had me scheduled on the weekends to work, so I just worked during the day, and then I would go to the church assigned for that night and sleep. Also; during this time, I thought that someday I would be the wife of Prince William of England. It was 2009 and tabloids showed him to be in a relationship with, now wife, Kate Middleton. Since I was 11 years old and watched the news of his mother's death, and saw a side-by-side picture of he and his brother Harry, I chose William. A feeling came over me like; I was destine to be a part of that family. I already had his Grandmother's name: Elizabeth; although Kate has the name too. His stepmother; Camilla, and I shared the same birthday: July 17. I have imagined his grandfather; Prince Philip, with the same sense of humor as me,

Chicago

cracking cruel but funny jokes on passerby's. As such; I took particular care on my reputation. I always thought before every major decision: *Would my reputation recover to be a wife of royalty if I do this or that*? And so; I not only didn't sleep with the cab driver for a place to lay my head but I was also securing my future as a royal. I figured poverty was understandable but prostitution...maybe not.

There were major differences I noticed between the shelters in Chicago's south suburbs and the shelters in New York. The diversity of people grouped together were one of them. In the New York shelters, the men were separated from the women, and singles from families. Here, everyone was grouped together. During the weekdays, everyone met at the day site, downstairs, in the yellow room. There was a kitchen, no stove, but one refrigerator where everyone kept their stuff. There were two computer rooms, a play room for the kids with a television box that you could only watch kid's movies on, and a common room with two one-seated couches. Upstairs had showers, but they were only open to us until 9a.m. In New York, showers were available all the time, unless it was being cleaned. I felt sorry for those with small children because together they had only the same amount of time as those who were single; which was fifteen minutes. There was even a timer in the bathrooms, wired to the lights that would shut off when our time was up. The upstairs area was where the case workers worked in their cubical offices, trying to check us homeless people into a permanent place of our own.

Like clockwork, we left the site at 6p.m. to arrive at the church assigned for that evening. There, they feed us and some churches entertained us with a movie. Then we were off to sleep on the church's basement floors with only a mat and some

After College When You Don't Have A Plan

blankets to separate us. In New York we were at least sleeping up high on a cot. Then at 5 or 5:30a.m. (Depending on which church we were at) they would wake us up, feed us breakfast, and then kick us out at seven in the morning to return to the site and take our showers. And after all of that, we still waited down stairs in the yellow room until it was time to do it all over again. Sometimes, the workers would come downstairs and do activities with us, but mostly we would sit in classroom desk all day, buying away the time. For those with a job, like me, that was a way of escaping the sadness of shelter life. I went out searching or looking in the paper every day for a place I could afford on an eight dollars and twenty-five cents per hour salary, promising only fifteen hours per week. I did not want to wait for staff at the site to find me something. Most of the people and families residing there had been there six months or longer without assistance, and there was not many of us staying there for it to be that way. In New York there were more than one hundred homeless single women, residing in one building. Here, there may have been thirty people including those with families. I was not about to wait six months or more to get assistance.

Within a month I found a couple of places but even a month of being there was far longer than I expected. Like New York, the rent here was too expensive on a single person's salary. Here it was four hundred and ninety dollars and up for a small studio in the suburbs. In the south suburbs of Chicago the rent was higher and this did not include the costs of utilities. I got paid every two weeks. Sometimes I would save almost my entire pay check toward future first month's rent and deposits. One day on my way in at the site from work I passed by a girl sitting upstairs in the lobby. I figured she was waiting to register and become one of us. She had on nice clothes and looked groomed and kept but so did we all. Since there were showers on the premises and nice

Chicago

clothes were donated to us, no one looked like the commercialized homeless person. Anyway, she gave me a number to call for housing for single homeless women working, and then I went down stairs. After that day I never saw her again. Looking back on it, I often wondered if she was an Angel sent from heaven just for me, if so, thank you. What appealed to me was the location. It was on the north side of Chicago. It was beautiful there. The area was close by Lake Michigan, my grandmother; Stepdad's mom lived near there. I always wanted to live in that area. In fact, in college I told all my friends I would live there someday, but I had given up hope that it would happen because it was far out of my price range. When opportunity presented itself I did not hesitate to call. During this time, a major holiday was approaching, Thanksgiving. My calls and business dealings would have to wait until after the holiday.

Thanksgiving was always a sad time for me because, since going away to college, I had always spent the holiday alone. This year was different. I had made some friends and was invited to a church where they were throwing a major dinner for the homeless in the area. Everyone was invited to come, homeless or not. That day was the best thanksgiving I had ever had. I had spent it with strangers, some whom I had only known for a couple of weeks. It was a great assurance to know that if personalities were to clash and spin out of control (like at most family holiday get-togethers), it would not affect me because they were strangers. The food and desserts were excellent. There was a buffet just for us and almost everyone was on their best behavior except for one homeless man hitting on an underage volunteer.

When the holiday ended things went back to where they were. As for me, I called the number that was given to me by the girl I never saw again. When I called, I was told the dealings

After College When You Don't Have A Plan

would have to go through my case worker and not me. I did not have a particular case worker because I worked; I was not recovering from a substance abuse issue, and I did not have a family so it was hard to put me into a category. Eventually, I was assigned to Kim, a housing director that is supposed to help get homeless people housing. Kim's personality was dull and unconcerned with how desperate I wanted out of my current situation. She reminded me of my first case worker in New York, Ms. Smith, where her only excitement was getting paid. That is how most of the case worker's personalities were, as though they had one too many people in need of their help and as a result they developed a shield over their feelings. The difference was that here they were not as verbally abusive, probably because there were kids present.

After much time pleading and convincing that this was an option, Kim made the call and set me up with an interview for an opening. I was so excited and everyone downstairs was excited for me too. Down there it was like family, everyone looked out for each other and made sure we all made it to the church sites to sleep. But like in any other family there was some backbiting. People downstairs would talk about you behind your back, but I was at work most of the time, I rarely got into what went on downstairs. On the other hand; no matter how family-oriented it was down there, it was not enough to make me want to stay.

When a month had passed and I was still homeless, I was at the end of my rope. It was now December of 2009. When the day came for the interview that Kim set up for me, I put my best foot forward. I did not let shelter life or any other problems I was going through upset me. When I arrived, a team of people were waiting to speak with me about an apartment. The apartment would be salary income-based. If I were to qualify I would only pay thirty percent of the rent and received a discount on the utilities. During the interview process I had to give a urine sample with a member from staff inside the restroom with me. I did not let the humiliation get to me. I told myself they were just checking for drugs. After the interview process was finished, I was expecting a date and time that I would move into an apartment, instead I was told that if I pass the interview process I would be put on their waiting list. After hearing that, I got deeply depressed.

When I went back to the Day Site everyone asked about how it went.

"Did you get the apartment?"

"When will you be moving in?" I had no good news that day. It seemed everyone resided at the Day Site. Like New York; old people, young people (that just made it to the legal adult age), parent with kids, the mentally disturbed, as well as physically-disabled people were all there, all grouped together. A young woman in her early twenties named Tiffany Wilkins, had just gotten out of the hospital after giving birth to her baby boy she named Malachi. Tiffany, along with her seven year old daughter named Heaven, who was then, just in the first grade, and Tiffany's mother, were all a part of the Day Site program. They too would go and sleep from church to church on the churches basement floors at night. She and her family had nowhere to go. I held her baby at ten days old in my arms. She told me her stitches had not even healed. She carried all those burdens. Weeks later I saw her picture and her story in a local newspaper called the *Southtown Star.* She mentioned that the shelter was nice to her but that she needed more help than nice words in her emergency situation. It took reporters and her story in the *Huffington Post* (Hattem, 2009) for she and her children to receive help. I did not

After College When You Don't Have A Plan

want to end up like that. I might not have been in the dire situation that she was in, but I wanted out of the shelter life as soon as possible.

The worst days were on Saturdays after leaving a church at 7a.m. The library did not open up until 10a.m. The temperature was always freezing and most of us were left to wander the streets until a public facility opened up. Some of the people were old, while others had to wander the cold streets with kids. There were times my sadness showed at work, but I refused to tell anyone about what was going on. I had only a little dignity, maybe it was from that five percent when I refused to sleep with the old cab driver for an exchange of a roof over my head on the weekends. Anyway; I got to know my day site buddies. One guy was a horny old man I called Grady because he reminded me of that character on Sanford and Sons. Even through his circumstances he'd always manage to flirt with me. I never entertained old Grady, but that never stopped him from trying. Grady was a senior and rehabilitated drug addict who always shared his wisdom with anyone who would listen. There were a couple of mothers with children there too; one in particular was my age of 26. Two of her youngest kids were with her at the site. They were the smallest and cutest kids there and were always ready to entertain. On the outside she seemed like a thug mom, about that life style. Although her kids were under the age of 3, she was either yelling or cursing them out. But; there were times I witnessed her protect her kids, made sure they were bathe and groomed to be the cuties that we were accustom to, and sometimes; when she thought no one was looking, would hug and kiss them. Opposite of Grady was an old and bitter Indian woman. At any given moment she could be found cursing someone out, it seem she enjoy doing this. Ironically; she and I got along perfectly. In-fact; I was everybody's go to favorite in the group. I witness all of their bottom lines as they witnessed mine while we struggled the shelter life together. No matter how hard times got it was a little comfort to me to know that I was not struggling alone; that there were situations that were worse than mines.

Meanwhile; I was ready to give up. I ran out of ideas on how to get out of my shelter situation. I had nowhere and no one to turn to. My case worker Kim met with me down stairs in the yellow room. She asked:

"What did you think about the interview you had for an apartment?" I told her that they put me on a waiting list. I also revealed that I was exhausted and had given up all hope that I would leave the shelter and get my own place. She said:

"That's too bad because they just called and told me that you were approved for an apartment." My jaw dropped, it was just a week since the interview and I was sure I would have a longer wait. Nothing but tears poured out of me. I couldn't even talk straight. Kim kept it professional though with a congratulations and a pat on my shoulder. My sadness turned into happiness when I got the news about the apartment. I got accepted and it only took a week.

That was the happiest day of my life.

It was now approaching Christmas and at that point I did not care what the apartment looked like, what neighborhood it was in, or what my neighbors would be like. I had finally gotten accepted into my own place. All I had left to do was sign some papers and collect the keys. Unfortunately I was scheduled to work on the day I was supposed to get this done. I was so desperate that I offered co-workers fifty dollars to trade shifts with me. But God works in mysterious ways because a guy traded places with me and I did not have to pay him anything. I was able

After College When You Don't Have A Plan

to get my apartment. They say if you can make it in New York (And I did, I did not get killed) you can make it anywhere. I made it to Chicago, Illinois to a beautiful apartment on the north side with pest-control, a beautiful view overlooking the park, and access to all the long hot baths I wanted. The apartment itself was more than I had ever dreamed of. First, the apartment was huge for a studio. It had new wood flooring, new wooden cabinets in the kitchen, and the kitchen was spacious, with marble flooring. The apartment came furnished. In the living room and bed room there was already a futon, a television with DVD and VHS set up, there were light brown oak-looking tables, all different sizes, set up around the apartment. One of the tables was used as an entertainment center to hold up the television and DVD player, and to store movies. The other tables were low and long, used to sit on. In the kitchen, I had a round wooden table and chairs to match. The only thing I had to bring in the apartment was a queen-size bed, and some pictures. The rest was already furnished. I did not know if things would be perfect from then on out and I did not know what the future would bring, but I did know that I was finally out of the shelters and into my own apartment.

The year turned into 2010 and for several months I had to travel back and forth to my job in the south suburbs until I could find employment where I lived. The total time it took me to travel from home to work and back again was six hours. Six hours of my life wasted into traveling. I had to take two trains and two buses in the winter season to make it to work. My exhaustion started to show and I could never seem to make it in on time. I was either a half an hour or a full hour late and it got the attention of my superiors. Also, I did not make enough money at work to travel back and forth, so there were nights I slept on the church's basement concrete floors all over again. I would stay overnight or

Chicago

sometimes days in the suburbs because I did not have enough money to make it home or I would miss that last bus on account of me working late. It was not something I could discuss with upper management; they were over filled with workers as it was. They were looking for an excuse to let people go, and I did not want to be one of them, so I suffered in silence.

It got so cold waiting for the bus or the train when I did have the transportation fare that my toes and fingers would go numb. Once I arrived to my warm apartment every fiber of my skin would just itch. I continued doing this for two months, until my body ached so badly that I had to quite. It was now the middle of February of 2010 when I quit my job and got my final pay check. I was terrified. I had no assurance that another job was coming. While I was employed, I sent in resumes and applications everywhere close to where I lived, but I got no responses. Just like before, when I moved in with my stepmother, my neighborhood was mostly family-owned business. There were no major grocery food store chains, like the job I just quite, for miles. Money ran out from my last pay check, so walking thirty-six plus blocks became a regular thing. I could not even afford two dollars and twenty-five cents to catch the bus or train to where the chain businesses were.

In March of 2010, I got a call for an interview at a sells store. I was so use to not hearing anything back, that when I put in for a job, it did not occur to me that I did not have an interview outfit. At that time, I was attending a church closer to where I lived on a regular basis. I was careful not tell anyone that I use to be homeless or was in need of anything. I was in a new area, no one knew me or knew where I came from, and I wanted to keep it that way. My dignity was slowly starting to repair itself and I did not want to make any mistakes. But I swallowed my pride and

After College When You Don't Have A Plan

asked the church for some clothes anyway, but they rarely donated women's clothing, so they gave me money from the church offering. I was so ashamed, I could not feel any lower. But I took it and bought a pair of pants. When it was time for the interview, I feared the guy who interviewed me could see my desperation for the job. I even made the mistake of asking about my pay, and I have never asked about pay during interviews before. I was taught in high school that asking that question is a reason for employers not to hire a person because it shows they are only interested in the money.

Because of this mistake and desperation I was not called back for a second interview and I did not get the job. On top of that, my rent was approaching, as well as the monthly utility payments. By the end of that week, with all the worries and stress I had on my shoulders, my hair was all over the apartment. I made a call to Pastor Aunt in Tennessee and she agreed to help me out with the rent. She also paid for a round trip ticket for me to visit and get away for a while. With my fortune looking the way it was, I took that offer in a heartbeat. When I got there in the middle of March of 2010, my main concern was making money. Unfortunately this put me back into a familiar setting; me, working all the time and barely making it. I went back to Tennessee, working the same temporary service jobs I left behind for a better opportunity. I even almost went back to working in a hotel as a maid, but I only had a week to stay. I couldn't help but think when I had a moment to rest, *where did I go wrong?* I am a four-year-college graduate, with no convictions, no priors, I am a decent citizen, got along with anyone I came in contact with, and I'm smart. Why were these jobs the only jobs I seem to be getting and the careers I was after got me a dead end? Sure; I could blame it on the economy, because Lord knows I have sent in so many resumes and applications, in so many alterations, that it's not even funny. I could place the blame in a lot of directions, but none of that was getting me a job.

When I left Tennessee and went back home it was approaching April of 2010. I paid my rent and a portion of my utilities with the money Pastor Aunt gave me. After paying those bills the money was gone. I did not have so much as a penny in my pockets. Meanwhile, I ran out of basic needed items, the food was running low, and there went my hair all over the apartment again from all the stress. On days when it was not so cold outside I went out looking for jobs, even at places I already applied to, only to get turned down again. Things got so bad that I sent out e-mails to various business owners, presidents of local colleges, and the city's alderman asking them to consider me for any job in their department.

Finally, I got a call for an interview at McDonald's and it was now May of 2010. This was my second interview in three months since I quit my job in the beginning of February. I was determined to get this job and nothing was getting in my way. When I arrived at the interview, there was a crowd of applicants all waiting for the opportunity to get the position. I did not care at this point that I was all dressed up in a skirt, pantyhose, and dress shoes for a McDonald's job; my goal was to get hired. When it was my turn to be interviewed, I acted calm, smiled, and threw in some humor. The next thing I knew I got a call back within a couple of hours telling me I got the job.

As happy as I was one would think I had gotten an executive job, I was so grateful. Finally; an income to pay my bills instead of wish money. I also talked with my counselors from the Housing Program, who helped get me the apartment. My interest was in going back to school for my Master's Degree. They thought it would be a great idea, so they scheduled me an

After College When You Don't Have A Plan

appointment to meet with a financial adviser to get grant money to go back to school. And the journey has not ended there. I might not have had a medical card, but, because I was in the housing program, I had free access to medical care for the first time since I left New York eight months ago. I had made an appointment to meet with a real doctor, instead of some nurse out of the emergency room, who was going to be my personal doctor. I had not had a doctor of my own since I was on my stepparents insurance.

It was around the end of spring of 2010 when I got my new test results. I asked all types of questions, reveled what the doctors told me in New York, and gave my new doctor all the paper work of my medical history that was given to me by my last exam. She concluded that I no longer had Trich (Trichomoniasis) or HPV (Human Papillomavirus). The doctor went on to say that she also treated me for Gonorrhea and Syphilis and all tests were negative. I had a normal Pap smear.

As far as what happened after I left the shelter life in both New York and in the south suburbs of Chicago; well, last I heard a few people made it out. Lauren, in New York, who also had a Bachelor's degree in Mathematics and a fire, took away her apartment; she moved from New York and in with a friend from Jersey. She now works and is seeking her own apartment. Ms. Smith; the just-there-to-collect a pay check case manager, she unfortunately still has her job. Ms. Rowe, the cynical case manager that helped and actually did her job, still works there as well and is in the process of moving into a new house as a first time home owner. Because of this expensive responsibility she is currently in the market of buying any ones food stamps off of them. As for the Day Site in South Chicago, they're still downstairs, sitting at a desk, waiting to transition to a church to sleep at for the night, then wake up at 5 or 5:30a.m. to do it all over again. Only a few people made it out from this tired regime besides me. A couple of families with kids were given apartments that paid seventy percent of their rent for the next two years while they saved up to pay the rent on their own. It was the same program that I was in with my apartment. Others from the Day Site broke down and went back to drugs and sleeping on the streets. The majority stayed at the Site until they were kicked out by management for not following the rules.

A Preacher from those churches we slept at overnights, once asked us:

"Why do we stay and what kept us there?" Some people said it was because they bond friendships with others and that they could not leave their friends behind. Others mention that the world was too cruel to go back into. Somebody said something about not being able to find a job to support themselves because of prior convictions. Those with families in the shelter seemed to have given up hope completely because they felt as though they disappointed their children. Bottom line, it just became too hard for some. Fortunately; for me, things were looking up. For the first time I could see the light at the end of the darkest and endless tunnel, and it felt amazing.

Well, after getting that McDonald's job, I got comfortable, too comfortable. The year was still 2010 and I was watching the Tyra Banks Show. Tyra Banks was a Victoria Secret model turned director over television and then had her own day time show that she named after herself. She had this male psychic on to predict the future for audience members according to their sign. This psychic looked directly into the camera and said:

"Cancers beware! This year expect to be pregnant." I was alone in the apartment when I said to myself; *after all I went*

After College When You Don't Have A Plan

through, there was no way I'm going to let some dude come in here and get me pregnant. I turned off the TV and dismissed the whole thing.

I was relaxed about my bills because of the McDonald's job, so I had time on my hands to reflect on my other needs. I worked as a cashier in the morning shift. I saw families, mostly Hispanics, get together and have breakfast every morning. I wasn't talking to my family. Stepmom kicked me out of her house and I hadn't spoken to her since, it had almost been a year. Stepdad was forever missing in action, my sisters Samantha and Beatrice lived in Chicago. Samantha lived the closest, but even when I got kicked out by our stepmom neither one of them would open up their doors to me. Samantha lived at the YMCA in a rent-a-room, but saved up and moved into a studio apartment near me. Beatrice and I had bad history.

Shortly after college; well, before Beatrice and I happen, I was still in college. My family and I had gotten evicted out of yet another house. So, Stepmom moved us into a hotel. Stepmom believes in God and makes it seems like she's holier than God. I mean, she'll take out her bible at work (she worked at a call center) and start speaking in tongues. But this same woman sat beside me on a bed in our hotel room, while she thought I was asleep, and whispered:

"I got a credit card in your name." She used my social security number and received a Sears credit card where my sister Beatrice worked, went to her counter, and exchange the purchases she made for cash. Fast forward; to after college, I go to a bank to open up a checking account and the bank tells me I already have a CREDIT CARD ACCOUNT open in my name. Whose telephone number is on the account? Beatrice's! So, I do some digging and it turns out Beatrice has opened credit cards as well as student loans all in my name. How could she be that bold?

Chicago

The government should not allow adolescences to possess a social security number until they are old enough to separate themselves from those who have easy access. Instead they should be given letters instead. Besides; there are more letters than numbers before it repeats itself. This way a child is identified as such more easily. Best of all, there would be no identity to steal. The letters given would be for the sole purpose of protecting under aged adolescence from parental or any other identity theft.

After Stepmom's whisper, I got up from the bed and went into another room, called the police, and was being given advice about how to fill out an affidavit. As a result, right then and there, Stepmom kicked me out of the hotel. Stepmom and I didn't speak for a while after that. So, I couldn't believe the arrogance that Beatrice would go behind what Stepmom did and basically do the same thing to me but on larger level. When I confronted Beatrice, despite all the proof, she denied it even to this present day. I called the police on my sister Beatrice that same day I found all of this out. We were both staying with Stepmom at the time, both just recent college graduates. Because Beatrice was paying Stepmom money and I wasn't, Stepmom told me to leave. I couldn't believe this; I was the victim and I was being kicked out. Meanwhile; Beatrice and what use to be my friend, then her boyfriend and now her husband, was waiting for me down stairs of Stepmom's apartment. Stepmom buzzed them in. Beatrice took a swing at me because I called the police, her face in raged! Meanwhile, I'm thinking: *But I'm the victim.* She ripped my favorite t-shirt off my chest while her boyfriend watched with much amusement. The cops came, made no arrest, and insisted that were family and should not be fighting. I got to my car; Stepmom met up with me, and did her famous whisper:

After College When You Don't Have A Plan

"If you tell the cops on Beatrice I will tell them you did it." I pushed Stepmom off my car and years later found myself living with her and my younger brothers and sisters after leaving the shelter in New York, only to be kicked out again.

But, now all that mess was behind me in the year 2010. I was at McDonald's seeing other families get along and eating breakfast together. I went reminiscing on the old college days and Facebooked a few exes and invited them over to my new apartment. At this time I was becoming a regular at the church who gave me the money to purchase the interview outfit. The members were either too old or too young for my age of 26 going on 27, so I didn't fit in, but I kept attending anyway.

The first college blast from the past wasn't an ex, as a-matter-of fact he didn't even attend my university, instead he was a friend of a friend. He came to my apartment with sex on his mind. I showed him to the door and he left my apartment the way he came: horny and untouched. That guy was never invited back. The 2nd was the first actual boyfriend I ever had: Seth. It was the week of his birthday in June. He lived with his mom at the time, but he drove hours out to see me. He too only had sex on his mind, but he made it less obvious, and unlike the other guy; we went out to dinner. I paid fifty dollars for our meals as a birthday present to him. He offered to pay, which was nice, but I dipped into the tithes and offing money to pay for it. We got back to my place and he spent the night. That evening he was urging me to sleep with him, but I just paid fifty dollars for our meals, he wasn't going to get the panties from me too. It was sometime in the early morning hours that I couldn't sleep, so I woke him up and used a condom to have sex with him. It was short and sweet and I was still wide awake. It had been more than a year since I had sex before giving in to him in that early morning. When the

Chicago

sun came up he rushed out like he had to be somewhere and I didn't see him again until years later. I took a pregnancy test afterwards and the test was negative as I thought it would be.

    The next blast from the past to show up was George, an old college lover. It was July of 2010 and he had walked for miles in the hot sun just to visit me; which I thought was sweet. He too lived with a relative: his grandmother and then with his cousin while trying to make ends meet. We got into a huge talk fight on his first visit to see me over what happened in college. When we were in college together I fell obsessed with my first sex partner. Things weren't working out so George came into the picture. I had an apartment off campus at the time and George made frequent visits to see me, but each time, he would leave my apartment the way he came: horny and untouched. Finally, George called me out of sexual frustration. I told him:

    "Rather you show up to my apartment or call me on the phone I'm still not having sex with you." Besides; I was not attracted to him. He was shorter than me and two years younger. George stopped me in mid-sentence:

    "Liz"; he called me-

    "We're not going to have sex." At this point I'm thinking: *You're right about that*. Then he says: "Instead we're going to make love." Next thing I knew he was at my place and we were making love all over that apartment, including the shower. Afterwards; I was confused. I still wasn't attracted to George but I like sleeping with him, while I still had unresolved feelings for my first obsession whom didn't love me back. So, I used George and told him I was pregnant to somehow gain the attention of my first lover. George and I went to a clinic's office so I could take a pregnancy test. When it showed negative I rejoiced in front of him. George's background involves DCS (Department of Children

After College When You Don't Have A Plan

Services) which he revealed to me as we were at the clinics office getting the test results. He said his mom dropped he and his brothers off at DCS when they were very young, then two years later his dad came and got them out of the system. I guess all of that came back to him, because on the ride back to the college dorms where he stayed, he started cussing me out.

So; it's July of 2010, he comes over, and we started arguing on his first visit because he told me he went behind my back and told people, who were my friends and who knew me, that I tried to trap him with a baby so he'll marry me. I always wondered why people in college approached me weird. Anyway, he came back to my apartment. He brought up sex and at the time I was in the mood for it, but I made it very clear: Not without a condom. So; there we were at the gas station. He staggered behind while I paid for the condoms. At this point my window for sex was closing, I felt low for being with a guy who couldn't even pay for a gas station condom. We went back to my place, and I had sex with him anyway. At one point he begged me to take off the condom, but the money I paid for the condoms was not going to waste so I told him:

"Hell No." When the sun came up he left, but he kept in constant contact with me by phone. George would always ask could he come back and the answer would always be the same: NO. Two weeks later George got me at yet another weak moment and asked could he come over. George walked even further out to get to me because he lived with another cousin this time. I walked outside to meet him at night and he was dripping with sweat. He came in, took a shower, and was in my underwear until his clothes dried. It started out with him giving me a massage and I swear I was determined that I would not have sex with him. He came over condom-less again and I swore to myself that I would

Chicago

not be the one to buy them. *That's the man's job*, I said to myself. He kissed me somewhere on my body during his massage, then held me close. At this point my body was completely open, but my mind was determined: *No condom, No pussy*. Then he begged:

"Please can I come in..please." As if he was speaking directly to my vagina and overriding my brain. My stupid vagina gave in and he was in there..condom-less. When the sun came up I woke up wanting more which never happens because I hate morning sex. Somewhere during, I swear this small voice in my head said:

"Stop now, you're going to end up pregnant." I said to this voice in my head:

"I don't care." This voice said back at me:

"You sure?" And I said:

"Yes!"

"Yes George!"

"Oh God yes!" I continued to ride the top of George to the melodies of Snoop Dogg and Robin Thicke's collaboration: It's In The Mornin'.

So, George got dressed and left, but he always called and stayed in contact. Meanwhile; yet another blast from the past showed up. He lived around the corner from me, but we always seemed to just miss each other in life. He too came up to the apartment with only one thing in mind, but he made it less obvious. The closes we got was dry humping each other. First; my sister Beatrice knew him from college, as did some of my friends, and I didn't want it leaking out that I was a slut. Second; he was cheap, he would eat out alone then stop by and tell me

After College When You Don't Have A Plan

about it. I was furious at him for that, but I kept it to myself. Lastly; he was a year or two younger than me. He made a great friend though; he would fix things around the apartment, sit with me during episodes of Sex and The City, and just talk with me. Something that I really wanted anyway, a companion instead of a sex partner.

It was now the end of August of 2010 and I was at a church members wedding drinking champagne when I notice a difference. When I drank there wasn't the normal gag reflex as when I usually drank strong alcoholic beverages. In the next few days I notice other abnormalities; such as, my period came one day and was gone the next, I was constantly dry around the vaginal area, and I had cramps like I was going to die. I used the Housing health services and made an emergency appointment to be seen and there I was told:

"It's positive."

I had just quit my job at McDonald's and now this. I quit my job because I figured I can do better. With the money I was making, I was able to take the bus and see businesses outside of walking distance. So; I put in applications at Currency Exchanges, schools, and colleges. I was sure with my educational background it would be any day now before I landed another job, so I quit my current job before I actually got a call back for a better one. Also; during this time, I was so emotional that I went off on everyone, even before the test results confirmed I was pregnant. I had an outer body experience, like: *What are you saying?* I even went off on the guy who fixed things around my apartment because he wouldn't take me out on a date. So as emotional as I was I called George only to have the machine pick up; Please leave a message:

Chicago

"I'm pregnant! You want me to have an abortion or what?" Before I could finish some female picked up the phone, which I later discovered was his cousin.

"Who is this?" she said.

"Is George there?" She ignores my question and continues to ask:

"Who is this?"

"Liz, a girl he knows." Then she says:

"No, he's not here." then hangs up on me. Two days later I got a call from George. So, there we were on the phone talking at last. I just came right out and ask him:

"Are you going to be there financially?" He says:

"I can't do that right now." I said something like:

"You did this to me on purpose." Then he chuckles and says:

"It's not mine I know what I did." At this point I'm outraged and I hang up on him in mid-sentence...click!

The next day I went back to the clinic's office and I was given only one option out of many. Before the pregnancy results I was a frequent visitor at the clinic for the symptoms I was having. I was asked many medical questions about my past history. At some point I told them I still sucked my thumb when stressed and pulled my hair out. Without an examination I was prescribed anxiety pills and a pregnancy test was not performed beforehand. I took them as prescribed that afternoon, passed out, and didn't wake up until the next day in the early morning hours. So, when it turned out that I was pregnant, abortion was the only conversation the clinic had with me. I felt like the odds were stacked against

After College When You Don't Have A Plan

me. I was living in housing where the rules were: I had to be single and working. They took a urine sample when I applied, not just to check for drugs, but also to see if I was pregnant. If found pregnant I would have to leave my apartment and be placed on a waiting list for another apartment. Meanwhile; where was my unborn child and I going to live? The father made it very clear he wasn't going to participate financially and he had denied the baby was his. I had no job now. I quit McDonald's before they fired me. My hormones were all over the place before I found out I was pregnant. I was forgetful, I cried one moment and was furious the next, and I was forever tired.

I was set up with a time and date: September 15, 2010, for the abortion procedure and it costs $50. I called a couple of my girlfriends from college. One, whom I had done the most for: Help throw her a birthday party at our favorite bar/club, got her a job with me working at Walmart, flew in to see her and her family on thanksgiving, and gave her money that she has developed amnesia to recall. She told me that she's with her man and said:

"I just introduced you two, you're stupid for still sexing the motherfucker!", and hangs up. Then I called Pastor Aunt in Tennessee and she said:

"Then he don't even deserve a child." and sends me $50 via western union.

Through all this I still attended church. On a Wednesday night I attended bible class. The members were put into groups according to their ages. My group was all women, much older than me. We went around the circle within my group giving a prayer request. When it was my turn I asked my group to pray for my sickness. Then one of the ladies pressed further in her questioning, so I reviled that I was pregnant and had no plans to

Chicago

keep it. No one said a word, but instead went on with the bible class for our group. Afterwards; the lady who pressed me with questions offered to drive me to the abortion clinic, she was insistent. She had 6 or 7 kids of her own and was going through a divorce. She picked me up as promised. On the way there, even while I stood in line in the dark early morning hours with 20 or so other women, she tried to talk me out of it, but my mind was set. I wouldn't even allow myself to doubt. My mind that day was totally centered for some reason. Usually, I look to the horoscopes to tell me what to do, but I was determined to go through with the decision to abort. So, she left, and there I was, standing in an open line outside, waiting to be called in.

    A heavy set female security guard came out and gave all us girls, standing in the dark-night-cold-air, numbers. I was almost at the front of the line. When we all got inside the building, we were called by the number assigned to us. I was called last to register. We were told by the receptionist not to eat anything for a couple of hours. I went to the cafeteria and ate green beans. The baby had me starving and it was only 8 weeks to the date. After all the questions and registering, the group of us patients had to wait until two that afternoon to pay our fifty dollars and get our abortions. During the time leading up to the day of the appointment; I pulled, then scissor cut my hair off because of the stress I was going through. So, when the group of us finally got called in I was mistaken for a boy. The other patients in my group were of different backgrounds and life styles, but they all had one thing in common that I didn't, they had at least one person by their side. One girl brought her whole entire family. Another was an older couple that said they had too many kids and couldn't afford the surprise baby. A younger couple; looked more like a pimp and his prostitute, had an arrogance about the whole thing, as though they'd been through

After College When You Don't Have A Plan

this before. But when we all as a group went into that room to get the procedure done, without families or significant others, confidence parted and sadness set in.

We were all instructed to take a pill to start the contractions. The nurse who gave the pills out said:

"Once you swallow there is no going back." And without a pause for consideration I swallowed. The group of us had already taken off our clothes and exchanged them for a hospital gown, with our belongings in a huge, brown, paper bag that was given to us. The room was all white, with black leather lounge chairs, complete with computer screen at each station. Behind all that were long white curtains, that groups of us sat behind, waiting to be called in, one-by-one by our number, when it was time for the procedure. Of course, I was the last one to be called. When I'm nervous, through no fault of my own, I tend to act goofy, child-like. The doctor came in and asked:

"Can you tell me why you're here today?" And I said in a child-like voice

"To get an abortion."

"That's right." the doctor said in amusement. I sat on a recliner table while the doctor used tools and the computer monitor to find the fetus

I almost got accustom to the fetus being in there to tell the truth. So far, I knew it had an expensive appetite. I was only getting $172 in food stamps every month. The baby craved sausages and I had to have the $7+ Home-Run-Inn sausage pizzas. It also liked hot lays potato chips and ginger-ale. Having the fetus inside me made me more assertive than I normally was. I had gone to the hospital to get an ultra sound because the clinic didn't have the equipment. I lived about 4 miles from the hospital.

Chicago

The old me would have just walked, in the late-night-cold-air, when I was finally released. I didn't have money for a cab. But that someone inside, turned me around, and I went back into the hospital and demanded that they send me for me a cab ride home. I told them to charge it to my bill that I had no intentions of paying for.

Once the fetus was located on the monitor, a suction was put inside me, and my assertive fetus was gone. Afterwards, I threw up. The assistant assisting the doctors yelled at me and said:

"We told you not to eat anything." I left the white, draped, curtain room and sat down on the black leather recliners. A nurse gave us group of girls' pain pills and checked our temperatures. They only gave us 25 minus a piece to sit and relax after the abortion. When I got up I felt as though my insides were going to fall through my vagina. I called the church member, who dropped me off, but her attitude became short tempered, so I called my grandma, my stepfather's mother who lived near me, and she sent her boyfriend André to pick me up. When he came he had $40 from my grandma to give to me. Because of the relationship I had with Stepmom, I didn't trust that the money was just given to me without any strings attached. I called her right then and there and assured her if I took it I can't pay it back. She said it was mine and André uncurled it from his hand to mine.

André didn't come up when he dropped me off at my apartment, which was on the top floor, and up three flights of stairs. The next day I was still sore but I needed groceries for the house. I went out shopping and came back bleeding. A couple of days later I went back to church, by this time that church member made her rounds, telling her friends that I got an abortion. I was not an official member because I still belonged to Pastor Aunt's

After College When You Don't Have A Plan

church in Tennessee. I was ganged up on one day after church. I was doing my rounds greeting everyone when that church member cornered me with the Pastor. And what could the Pastor have said, a man and not a woman? All he said was that we'll talk, but we never did.

During this time, a couple my age was new to the area and joined the church. They'd invite me to dinner, other church programs, offered free car rides to the store, and best of all they didn't know about the abortion. Also, they attracted others our ages to visit each other's homes and host a meal. For a while it was fun. One day on my way to church to return some movies I borrowed from the couple, a huge screen was put up and the Pastor's sermon was on abortion. There was a teen couple pregnant at the church who decided to have their baby. While I tried to hide what I'd been through with a smile and a happy disposition, to them I guess I was seen as a hypocrite. The young teens where kicked out their homes when their parents found out and the Pastor allowed them to live in his home until he could find housing and a job for the teenage father-to-be. Here I was; with the decision to abort, living in an apartment to myself, overlooking the park, and always seemed happy with a smile on my face. So, during the Pastor's sermon he put up pictures of dead fetuses and told the congregation, looking directly at me, that women who have abortions don't love their babies. Looking back, his sermon was one sided and from a man's perspective only. I believe I made the appropriate choice by not bring a child into this world. I could not just hope for the best. My stepparents did that with their kids. I don't remember a time when we weren't on public assistants. Stepmom remarried and moved us into fancy neighborhoods we couldn't afford and eventually got kicked out of. She always secured the finances. She would brag constantly and tell my sisters and me to marry a man whose going to bring

Chicago

home his whole check over to his wife and allow her to give back to him what she wants. Once; in the third grade, my sisters and I got off the school bus to find Dean, another Stepdad, placing the last of our things back inside the home we were being evicted from. Stepmom was nowhere to be found; although, some say she was out shopping with her best friend Ms. Jones. Stepmom was notorious for leaving early in the mornings and returning late at night. Dean never stood up to her; at least not in-front of my sister's and I. Stepdad; I could only imagine, was somewhere laughing. He and Stepmom had always been in a financial competition from what I've witness growing up. So; when Stepmom got that house, got full custody of my sister's and me, along with a brand new husband willing to take all of us in as his own, Stepdad was pissed with envy. The Sheriff showed up along with the police in-front of everyone in our neighborhood. My sister's and I was put in the back of a police car. A woman officer yelled:

"Shut up!" at us when we cried. We were driven to Dean's family's house and that's where I learned the cute trick of putting a treat in my hands, putting my hands behind my back, and then with closed fist, present my hands forward, not revealing the treat inside, making my contestant choose which fist carried the treat. A game played on me by Dean's brothers. It was a good distraction from what I'd just gone through. I didn't see Stepmom or her family, Stepdad and his family, the only people who was there when it counted were strangers.

Pastor Aunt, Stepmom's sister, would make an appearance from time-to-time. To me she represented a beckoning force against Stepmom. Pastor Aunt brought my sister's and I our first pair of name brand shoes: black and white Nike's. I wouldn't get another pair of name brand shoes until after college. Stepmom

After College When You Don't Have A Plan

disliked it when her sister challenged her authority, but I was grateful for it. Her husbands couldn't even stand up to her. Pastor Aunt was that safe haven who came into my sister's and I lives when no other family members would because it wasn't worth the hassle to deal with our stepmother.

The day after, I saw Stepmom. We all moved into her best friend's house and she made my sister's and I go right back to the same school with kids in our neighborhood who saw us being evicted. Tyson White; a boy I liked, made fun of me. I just stood there and said nothing, setting myself up for future responses towards humiliating situations. Bottom line; I didn't want my unborn child to suffer my sister's and I same childhood, and I did not want to end up like Tiffany Wilkins. Her story was on the front page local newspaper showing her daughter Heaven looking away while Tiffany held her recent newborn just to get housing assistance during the cold months in the south suburbs of Chicago. Before bring any children into this world I felt a personal obligation to give them a running start.

After his sermon I walked the neighborhood and cried. Shortly after; the married couple distance themselves from me, as well as others in the church, so I stopped going. Everything in the apartment reminded me of my short comings. I packed my things and just left. Housing was furious, asking:

"What happen?"

"How could you just leave?" As one would ask-

"How could this have been prevented?" The program did all that they could. They set me up with a beautiful pets control apartment, assigned a case worker to drop by to check in on me, and they were in the process of setting up a program so that I could go back to school. I was grateful to the members of this

Chicago

program for picking me, out of a bad situation. For me, I was lonely, and although my case worker stop by every once and a while and I attended church, there wasn't a familiar face and I couldn't leave the past in the past. I was stuck where I left off before the homeless situation started happening; which was back in college. Psych exams are given during the screening process, but if someone is giving you hope out of a dead end situation only to take it away if you don't answer the psych questions in a way that *passes*, then nobody wins. I think it would have helped me to talk to a psychiatrist, but nobody listens for free and there were no programs for that just medication. Also; I didn't have what's called a *profitable nitch,* something I do well that makes money. When I graduated college I had no clue what to do to earn a decent living for myself. Now, I see why interning and school field trips are so important. One; It gives you a glimpse of what careers are available, Two; promotes thinking and interest in different career fields, lastly; it helps a person understand what they do and do not want from a career. While I was attending elementary, grade, and high school they had already cut out activities such as field trips, and when I did go, it was to the zoo or football stadium off season. I did intern for a law firm during college, but it was only for college credit. I admit it was laziness on my part. Now that I see its importance: To meet prospective employers, build a relationship with managers that can help put me into a position, and to sell myself into the career I wanted. I should have did more than I did. Instead; I worked straight through college, missing the experience entirely. I probably wouldn't have been in my situations if I had plan more rather than just graduating and hoping for the best. Bottom line, I messed up and by moving out it was my way of starting over on a clean slate.

After College When You Don't Have A Plan

COMMENTS

Leave a comment...

John1294

She's moving again? No! She should stay and build on what she has, like a rent controlled apartment.

Vicky127

John1294 No, she shouldn't stay. She no longer has a job. Even rent control costs money.

Chicago

John1294

Vicky127 Then where is she suppose to go?

Elizabeth Rochelle FeelJoy

Everyone keep reading

BACK TO TENNESSEE

Chapter 4
Back to Tennessee

I went back to Tennessee and lived with Pastor Aunt again. I got a job right away at Walmart. I got an unexpected call from the couple I hung out with in Chicago. They wanted information about my apartment to move the pregnant teens in, no concerns about me. I gave them a number and never heard from them again.

While I was in that apartment and after the abortion, I filled out job applications everywhere. I got hired with Sears, the oldest store still standing on Lawrence Avenue's Lincoln Square, as holiday help. After the holidays they still wanted to keep me on, but I was having health issues. I still put in applications for sit-down positions with higher pay, but I got no reply. So, here I was again in Tennessee and working my old college job: Walmart. I was on a mission. I would work to save up for a car. Tennessee didn't have Chicago's public transportation system. All they had was the bus and any and everybody could take a ride including the crazy's. My next mission would be to move out as soon as possible into my own place because it's nothing like having your own. The plan to go back to school set up by the Housing program got put further on hold, besides I still didn't know what I was good at to turn into a profit other than working for chain businesses. I had a lot of great ideas, but it required money I didn't have and stability which I had yet to conquer.

Back to Tennessee

The New Year came and it was 2011. I was deeply depressed after the abortion when I arrived in Tennessee, not because I thought I made the wrong decision, but because everyone around me was having babies. I was too poor to have kept mine. I ran into Tony. I met Tony earlier on when I first came to Tara, TN, after college, while I was in a relationship with that old guy who was older than both my parents. Tony was much older than me too, but my parents had at least one year on him. Tony wanted me back then but I had nothing to do with him. We would jog together, and all I saw him as was just a friend. When he wanted more I backed off. So, here it was, spring of 2011 and I'm not with the old guy and Tony was single, but after everything I'd went through I wanted to be alone. At the time he'd just found Jehovah as a Jehovah's Witness, got a new and steady job, and won partial custody of his daughter. What I didn't know was that he'd just gotten out of jail after doing five years for aggravated assault against his then pregnant girlfriend when I first met him to go jogging. He was also homeless until his involvement in a car accident won him legal fees. By the time I'd arrived back on the scene, the courts had just granted Tony permission to take the breathalyzer out of his car for a past DUI (Driving under the influence) charge. I had no idea of this, but every fiber of my instincts urged me to stay away.

Although I was focused on getting my life together I secretly wanted to be wined and dined. When I was in Chicago I would see mom's drop of their kids at fancy catholic schools, pulling up in the latest model SUV, dripping with diamonds and fur coats. Then; there was me, a poor bum in a fancy neighborhood. I didn't want to believe that that would never be me. That's why my situation didn't keep me from wanting those nice things, lavish life styles, and husbands like theirs that cared enough to secure his family in that way. By now, it had already been confirmed that Prince William married his girlfriend Kate Middleton. I should have known, they looked so much alike. Couples that look-a-like remain married until they die. I still couldn't shake the feeling that I belonged in that family so I kept hope for Prince Harry instead. I even went as far as to look up the meaning of his sign on: Howstuffworks.com. Under: Friends and Lovers; he is a Virgo who likes to surround himself with attractive people who makes him feel good about himself; yet, when he meets his soul mate he will be surprised that this person in no way *jibes* with his ideal. Reading this, I instantly thought: *he's going to marry a black lady, and that black lady is going to be me*. This made me further insist on me getting my life together and presenting me in a way fit for a royal.

"When a man wants something he'll stop at nothing to-get-it" Stepmom once said. Tony wore me down until I'd finally agreed to go out with him. Showing up to my family's functions and my family having a positive reaction towards him is what made me give in. So, at that point I now knew about his past and in return he now knew my baggage with the abortion, experiencing homelessness, and even my medical history. We were at a restaurant talking about us getting into a committed relationship when I let Tony know that I had never been hit before and if he were to hit me; right then and there I would leave him and never go back. Because of both our renewed commitments to our own separate faiths; his, a Jehovah's witness and mine, a Christian. We also made a promise not to sleep with each other before marriage.

For a while the courtship was wonderful. Every weekend was date night, we danced, we dinned, and Tony even brought me roses for no reason. I think he was at a point in his life where he

Back to Tennessee

just wanted to make his wrongs right with somebody and I just happen to walk in the picture. What I wouldn't give to get into a situation like that again. None-the-less, I didn't appreciate Tony. He had an image of me that, no matter how mean I was to him, it was hard for him to react to who I was in the present, but eventually he did. One night I came over to his place. By this time we were already sexing and cursing each other out, all while still going to church. We were in his bed having sex. I came, was tired, and ready to rest. Tony; on the other hand, was persistent to go further. He held me down and gave me this look, like if I got up he'll hit me. Ironically; I didn't feel any pain as one would if being rapped. My body enjoyed it but I didn't and I didn't even know that was possible. Afterwards; I cried and he cradled me asking what's wrong. I told him I didn't want what he just did to me; he just did what he wanted without my permission. At this point he says:

"No, no." Then I tried to leave out the door but he blocked it and motioned me to the couch to sit down and talk. Tony then tells me he came inside of me.

"Why did you do that?" I said.

"So you'll stay." he says. For weeks I had been making plans to leave him. The fairy tale courtship started to disintegrate. Tony would show up at my job to the point of stocking me. He even showed up with a prescription bag, claiming I gave him an STD, little did he know I had already just had a checkup before we were physical and I checked out fine. After his scene I went to the clinic he got the prescriptions from to have myself checked again. Turned out Tony had only told them he's got an STD from his girlfriend, and he was never given an exam only medications to treat the symptoms. Finally; I just had to quit Walmart and work someplace else, but he found me there too.

After College When You Don't Have A Plan

The reason that I have never been hit was because I never stayed in relationships long enough. The first sign of trouble is when I would bolt.

At that point he finally allows me to leave and I literally ran back to my car that I had saved up to buy. I went back to Pastor Aunt's house, I still lived there. I went to my room and thought to myself: *what if he got me pregnant*? So, I went out to Walgreen's Drug Store that nigh and ask for the Plan B pill that had just come out, advertised on commercials everywhere. The clerk said it'll be $50, the same costs of the abortion I had 11 months earlier. I weighted my options, and I had none, decided to buy it, and swallowed. I left Tara and it was back to square one. I had no direction and nowhere to go when I hit my foot on the gas pedal. I just needed to get out of there before the situation between me and Tony got worse and God forbid, bring a baby into the world.

Back to Tennessee

COMMENTS

Leave a comment...

Jackie1workaholic

The last thing she needed was a relationship.

John1294

Jackie1workaholic I couldn't agree more.

Miketheman

How is she thinking she's supposed to end up with the Prince of England but she's messing around with less than?

After College When You Don't Have A Plan

Vicky127

Miketheman I know right.

BigPaul

Miketheman Exactly!

Elizabeth Rochelle FeelJoy

To everyone So far have you put the author's choices into your own perspective's? There's more, stay tune and keep reading

BigPaul

Elizabeth Rochelle FeelJoy I'm getting tired of your: *stay tune and keep reading,* day time soap opera! Does the author come up on something or not?

Back to Tennessee

Miketheman

BigPaul I feel the same way. I'm ready for her to win the lottery or something.

Suzanne Merriweather

Reading so far, it appears she needs to pick a state and just stay there, for better or for worse. She started off this journey in 2007 at age 24 and now it's 2011, so she's 28.

Vicky 127

Suzanne Merriweather Omg! You're right.

John1294

Suzanne Merriweather Damn!

STATE

TO

STATE

Chapter 5
State-to-state

I ended up in Nashville, east of Tara. I had some money on me so I rented a hotel for a week. Meanwhile, I tried to find a job, but if you don't have a physical address or don't know someone's address, then jobs won't call back for an interview. Also; If you don't have check stubs then apartments won't approve you. So, here I was stuck in-between catch 22 as Stepmom use to say. As luck would find it, my cousin Connie lived in the projects in Nashville.

Connie had 5 kids under the age of 9, and lived with an abusive, unfaithful, baby's daddy number 4. Despite all that, she still open her door to me for the low price of $60. That night a S.W.A.T team of police banged on her front door, beamed abrasive flashlights through the window, and on a loud speaker for the whole projects to hear; an officer threaten my cousin that if she didn't open the door they were going to take away her kids. I personally have never came close to being in trouble with the law, but I knew what the cops were doing to my cousin and her family was unlawful; so I called the police station and alerted them of the matter. Next thing I knew the spread of cops that were there were packing up and driving away. After this happened I knew I couldn't stay there. I didn't want my cousin staying there either, being subjected to police cruelty, but there was nothing I could do for her except save myself.

I got another hotel room, and then I got a temp job that lasted for just one day. I took my earnings and headed north. I ended up in St. Louis, Missouri before the car gave out on me. I

State-to-state

let it cool down, prayed to Jesus like I've never prayed to him before, and then the car started back up. I looked on Craigslist and found a cheap rented-a-room. I wasn't hassled about having a job and references; just pay rent on time was all that was required. During that time, Tony kept in touch with me via phone and we were arguing every day. I was too young for what he wanted me to commit to. Tony was 18 years older than me and by then I was only 28 years old.

    I shared a house of rooms with a 50 year old white man named Tim, who lived down stairs and a 60 year old black lady who lived upstairs in a room across from mine. I liked it there because I always had a roommate to talk to and when I wanted to be alone I could always retreat to the solitude of my room. Times got hard. I found a job at a retail store, but had to quit because of the pain of standing on my feet for hours. Tim earned money by doing clinical trials for medicine. He took me there, next thing I knew I was doing the trails too. My first one was testing a new pain medication. I remember having to stay overnight for a couple of nights. Blood was drawn from me on a consistent basis. I was a part of a large group. We were fed 3 meals, but weren't allowed to do physical activities or leave the study. I always felt sick but I was afraid if I showed it they would dismiss me from the study and that I wouldn't receive my whole pay. At the end of the study I received a $600 check for just a couple of days. I tried to enter another study but my body was just too weak. So; money ran low again. At this time I kept in contact with my sister Samantha who moved to Quincy, IL just an hour away from St. Louis. I told her I couldn't afford the rent anymore and she quickly became my next move, I was packing up and moving in with her. This was during Thanksgiving. Neither one of us could

After College When You Don't Have A Plan

cook or felt like attempting, so we went to a Free Meal Event and enjoyed the holidays with strangers.

At times Samantha scared me. She knew I was broke and had nowhere to go, but she would say things like:

"I need dick!" In other words it was time for me to go, or just pick fights with me for no reason. Back in college Samantha did stay with me when I had an apartment off campus. We had an argument about her getting a job to help pay for expenses. She'll say everyone in town was prejudice and didn't want to give her a chance and I argued against this. At that point she started cussing me out, so I told her she had to go. I wasn't concern where she went because she had hurt my feelings. Fast forward to now and I'm living in her apartment where I guess this was payback. Through it, I kept my head down and my mouth shut while working a part time job she set up for me. Also; during that time, Tony and I were to a close on whatever we were in our long distance relationship. I remember calling him up and saying he was too old and needed to find someone his own age. I was bored and I hadn't heard from him, but looking back, I didn't mean those things I said. At the end of our conversation he was quiet and I knew exactly what that meant.

Shortly after graduating college I went through similar circumstances with an ex college lover I couldn't shake off. I was living in Chicago in the Housing program at that time when one day, out of the blue, he called me twice and only in the mornings. By that second call when he asked:

"Why don't you live with your parents?" and my response was:

"I'm a grown up.", he too got quiet. He was looking for more than just a catch up, he was at a cross roads in his life.

State-to-state

Before I uttered the response I understood completely the situation within that second, but the words fell out of my mouth at full speed ahead. As a result that young man got married and it wasn't to me. Now Tony and it was dejavu all over again. I called a couple of days later and he said:

"I'm out with my lady." and hung up on me. It was over.

When I had enough money in my pocket for gas, I packed up just after New Years of 2012 and headed for California. During this time I was trying to finish this book you're reading now. Given the stress I was under living at my younger sister Samantha's apartment, I psyched myself up to believe fate wanted me in California where publicists were. Samantha begged me not to go, but I couldn't take one more minute of her unstable personality: love me one second, hate me the next. I was all gas up and heading west. Somewhere between New Mexico and Arizona I ran out of gas money. During the whole trip I slept, ate, and used the bathroom near the car. I called Stepmom in Chicago and to my surprise she wired me money on more than one occasion. It took me a week almost to drive from Illinois to Los Angeles.

It was now February 2012 and as I approached the western coast the weather got hot and hotter, especially driving through Arizona. When I arrived in California Stepmom had already prepaid a motel with a week's stay in Gardena, about 23 miles from Hollywood. Arriving in California, I could already tell that this was a bad decision. Upon arriving at the motel my first instinct was to find work so that at the end of seven days I won't be on the street or sleeping in my car. Oddly enough no call backs and no one was hiring. Every day that I woke I prayed to God and thanked him for giving me another opportunity on earth. The Library became my permanent hang out spot to look for work.

After College When You Don't Have A Plan

It wasn't all search for work and no play. I drove to a nearby beach only to discover it was being rehabbed on. One side of the beach had construction going on. Then, on the other side was a small space for the public. The weather was tricky too. The temperature would go up and down throughout the day causing me to get sick. I went window shopping at the Kodak Theater and the clothes were cheaper than I've seen on Central or Eastern coasts. I saw the HOLLYWOOD sign and nearly died in amazement. One day while visiting the Kodak Theater, it was hosting an Awards show. I saw workers quickly lay down the red carpet just minus before Hollywood celebrities got out to walk it. It was wired to see it live and up close through the steel gates set out by security and police. The red carpet was drawn in the middle of a rundown area, but the cameras captured only the glamour set up that I was used to seeing on television. Meanwhile; my time at the motel was coming to an end and I needed to find a job quickly.

One day in February, I was standing in line at the library, waiting to use a computer. Hanging the walls, I saw pictures of famous musicians who had passed on and one of Whitney Houston. I thought to myself: *that's not right, she doesn't belong up there, she's not dead.* I went back to my motel room and next door I heard a man shouting:

"Whitney Houston is dead!" I turned on the TV and sure enough all the reports confirmed. Her lifeless body was just 30 minutes from me and I wanted to go see for myself. In high school I can remember getting into a fight with some girl because she teased, Whitney Houston was on drugs. Back then I refused to believe it. As much as I wanted to be there, even if that was just outside of the Beverly Hills Hotel, my finances wouldn't let me do it. I was low on gas, my car was leaking oil, and I thought the police would have surely taken the body away before I even got there. Whitney Houston's body stayed in that hotel overnight.

State-to-state

There was even a party held a couple of floors down from her hotel room where she still remained.

Despite the shock from the previous day I still needed a job and I had only a couple of days left. Every night I cried and prayed:

"God please don't let me leave this hotel only to go live in my car again.", but that's exactly what happened. I was still thankful God gave me another day. There was a day site called P.A.T.H (People Assisting The Homeless) in Hollywood, California. They selected a few homeless to live on the premises. Others, like me, was only allowed to use their services (showers, phone, and job search logs) during the day and sleep elsewhere at night. I slept in my car. Outside of the Hollywood sign, the Kodak Theater, and the beaches, Los Angeles, California itself was depressing. It was filled with homeless people and sadly I was one of them, sleeping in my car, and going to the day site for showers Monday-Friday because they weren't open on weekends.

Luckily; the temp service I used in Tennessee seemed to be universal in every state and to my surprise there were several branches in Los Angeles. In every branch I had to sign paper work all over again as though I was new. After I signed and passed a safety test, they gave to every incoming new applicant, I waited in their lobby, sometimes as early as 5:30am to get sent out on an assignment. I waited with people from all walks of life, but mostly with homeless men. My need for money relaxed any fears about being in that situation. I didn't engage in prostitution; what might have been an easier way to get money. I was a college graduate, with my own car, who was just trying to find my place in the world. Thoughts of that nature didn't even occur to me because in many ways I still felt above the rest. To this day I'd rather use my hands or my mind for money rather than my body

After College When You Don't Have A PlanS

exually; nothing against women who do this but it was not for me. Besides; I always imagined the sex being different in the worst way when one is being paid to do so. After I passed the safety test it took 4 days of me showing up every morning before I was finally sent out on an assignment. Out of all those men my name was called. It was for a weekend job as a sign holder for a cell phone company. When your name is called it can make one feel like the luckiest person alive, no matter where the company might have sent me. I parked my car next to the location I was assigned to work. There; I slept, then sprayed myself clean and worked my weekend job with pride. I didn't get sent on another job assignment after, but I continued to wait in their lobby with all the rest of the unemployable. Thank God I had food stamps at the time. If I wasn't waiting on a job or finding places to park and sleep, I was shopping for groceries that didn't require a refrigerator. My car was my home and the passenger seat was my kitchen. Surprisingly enough I kept a clean and orderly car. One day coming from the grocery store I found a note on my car saying: *If I'm interested in selling call the number on the note.*

    A week after showing up at the temp service with no work assignment prospects, I went to Craigslist to find work. I got a call back to work in a call center in Upland, California convincing businesses to use our business as their ink and cartilage supplier. I got hired and was paid a check on a weekly basis. It was now March of 2012 and I still haven't secured a permanent place to live let alone found a publicist to publish my unfinished 19 page book; the reason I came to California in the first place. I had a job so I felt as though I was on the right track. It paid just 8.50 per hour, but I was promised 40 hours a week, equaling $340 per week. When I got my first pay check I checked into a hotel which costs $50 for a night's stay. No matter how much I tried to save up to get a place I always came out broke by the end of the week.

State-to-state

I went back to the day site P.A.T.H and let them know I now had a job. Immediately they set me up with a shelter on Cortner Avenue in Los Angeles, 1.5 hours away from my job in Upland. Upon arriving I hit the back of my car trying to park in their garage and I wasn't allowed to bring any outside food or water into the building. As always it was a long and tedious process to register. Once I signed all the paper work and was explained their rules, they allowed me to eat, then showed me to my cubical. I was up against a brick wall painted white with a cot to sleep on. There were rows of cubicles going down with a row facing me. This was a unisex shelter. Men were in a door way on one side while women were on the other side of the door. We would all have daily meetings in the kitchen, but because I worked I was often times excused. The disciplinary team leader was a good looking man in his 30's. One day after coming home from work I ran out of gas. He came to where I was and helped me. I don't know if one of the workers spoke to him, but shortly after, in a kitchen meeting, he lectured about staff's duties and that it was not to personally assist the homeless. The timing couldn't be more unfortunate because I had developed the flu. I took the ambulance to the hospital. When I called the shelter and got him on the line, he told me to get a cab that I had to pay for out of my own pocket.

It was now April of 2012 and finding an apartment I could afford seemed bleak. A studio under the day site P.A.T.H program was $580 per month, plus deposit. I put myself on a waiting list for public housing outside of P.A.T.H.'s program and tried to sign myself up for section 8 housing but the list was closed by the time I arrived in Los Angeles. Because of the flu I was taking more time off of work, which meant less pay. Finally; I just gave up and left that shelter and went back into my car where ironically I didn't get sick.

After College When You Don't Have A Plan

It was income tax season time, the best time of the year and my check was due in May. Now that I was back in the car I used the day site again for early morning showers and public information. Besides; In the car I didn't have to follow nobody's rules, or have to be back by a certain time, or have staff just watch as I struggled with the flu while getting groceries for myself because I couldn't eat the food they served. Day to day it was a stretch on my mental and physical capabilities. Despite it all I still showed up to work dressed in decent attire and clean. When I couldn't get to the day site, because they were closed on the weekends, I'd wash up in a store's or restaurant's restrooms with single occupancy. The hardest thing to do while living in the car was finding places that will let you use their restrooms for free. Not even gas stations allowed non customers to use the facilities, but once I found a place, I would used it until they put up that notorious: OUT OF ORDER sign, then it was back to square one.

Eventually I quit my job too. It became too exhausting driving almost 2 hours back and forth from the day site and having to be at work by 6a.m. I quickly looked for other jobs with housing benefits but found none. Luckily, my income taxes came through. I gas up the car and headed back Midwest. I thought in a big city like Los Angeles, employers would at least pay more to its employees, but their minimum wage was the same as the central and eastern cost in 2012. The city was crowded with homeless people. One day; while walking pass a bench filled with newspaper, an old white lady emerged from the papers with blue lips begging me for a cigarette. I didn't smoke so I told her I did not have a cigarette. The cycle of getting a job and a place to live was hopeless. Funding was cut all over the place as told by staff at P.A.T.H. I left and landed in Corpus Christie, Texas where that

State-to-state

famous singer Selena was killed by her accountant. As a kid I watched her movie hundreds of times but it did not occur to me that she was from there. I wanted to be near the water and this city was the closes spot to it.

After arriving; I checked in to another shelter. This was a real shelter for women and children only, where I could also sleep inside the premises. I was assigned a room with a curtain for a door to share with 3 other bunk mates. There were 2 bunks to a room and each bunk had 2 beds, one on top and the other at the bottom, just like a dorm room in college. The bathroom held several showers and restrooms. Unlike the shelters I experienced before, this was a small group of 10-15 singles and families. Corpus Christie is a small town compared to the cities I've been to. It was just one shelter building for men and women with children in town with two sides to it. Just about everyone in town had a job, home, and a family. The types of people who lived in this shelter were abused woman and new arrivals to the city like me. The staff and their attitudes were the same though. I met with a intake specialist; duties much like a social worker, to register. She was in her early forties and bragged that she was just finishing up her Associates degree in social work. During discussing the rules she told me:

"If the rules are not followed then I will be sending you back to your little car.", then giggled to herself. Thankfully; the other staff members were much kindhearted. Shockingly; my attitude during this time was less than perfect too. I was snobbish, self-centered, and I looked down at people in my surroundings. The overall people I interacted with were non-threatening and needy. I was the youngest person at the shelter with a car and wore a pretty wig. Now; when I look back on it, I'm embarrassed and can only imagine what I came across as, to others, during that time.

While there I decided to look into A&M University. One night, out of the blue, I started to re-evaluate my life and what direction it was headed. Up until this point I wanted to publish my 19 page book or write a couple of hit songs and become a millionaire or the next Amy Winehouse. I already had a Bachelor's degree in Communication, but so far the jobs for my field of news anchors and journalist were closed by the time I graduated. My cousin Valarie was a teacher and hated her job, but I was more thick skinned then she was. So; I made an appointment to meet with the school's counselor and enroll for a 2nd bachelor's degree as a teacher. Somewhere between applying for school and waiting for my meeting with the career counselor, I also had my palm read for the very first time. Based on my palm the reading, I packed all my things, missed my appointment with the career counselor, and op-out of my student admission fee. I was headed back to where it all started: Tara, TN.

COMMENTS

Leave a comment...

State-to-state

Lacy Hamilton

A palm reader? But she has a Bachelor's degree. I can't imagine those things come cheap.

Suzanne Merriweather

Well; going to all these places, at least she got to see St. Louis, witness Whitney Houston's death, and visit Selena's home town. How old is she now?

> Jackie1workaholic
>
>
>
> Suzanne Merriweather 29!

>> Miketheman
>>
>>
>>
>> Jackie1workaholic SMH (Shaking my head).

After College When You Don't Have A Plan

BigPaul

Miketheman Same

John1294

I hate to say I told you so, but like I've been saying, the grass is never greener on the other side. She should have stayed where she was at way back in New York.

Lacy Hamilton

John1294 Where she got sexually harassed? No.

John1294

Lacy Hamilton Hell; she's sexually harassed all over this story.

State-to-state

Elizabeth Rochelle FeelJoy

Are good times ahead? Continue reading.

BACK TO TENNESSEE PART 2

After College When You Don't Have A Plan

Chapter 6

Back to Tennessee part 2

When I got there, however; Tara was not welcoming me back with open arms, not that it ever did. Instead, I got the police called on me multiple times for parking my car on private property to sleep. Sure; I could have went back to Pastor Aunt's place, but I was determined to make it without her. Instead, I went further out into the country to visit that old guy who was older than both my parents. He was conveniently out of town visiting relatives when I arrived. So, I gave a surprise visit to my ex Tony. It was about 10' o clock at night when I showed up at his door step. I was hoping he'll take me in so I wouldn't have to sleep in the car. When I arrived, at first he looked stunned. He let me in. He wore just a robe. Then he shifted his robe, revealing his erected penis. I was not in the mood and if I'd slept with him that night I would be nothing more than the cheapest prostitute, looking for free room and board, all with a bachelor's degree. So; I walked out, leaving him with a hard-on.

To my surprise I did find a shelter in Tara. It was more like a rehab; one of the requirements was that you can't leave the premises to get a job or anything for a couple of weeks. Also; you had to attend an in-house church on a daily basis. On the hind sight, they gave me my own room, everything was free, and I was out of my car. That all ended when the house manager demanded I put on a bra. I got offended; of which I was in no position to do so. I packed my things and was back in the car. Luckily; there

Back to Tennessee part 2

was another shelter in Tara. This time it was in a large mansion own by a white man who lived upstairs with his family, the homeless stayed downstairs. The rules were much more relaxed as well. I could leave to go search for work there.

I found a sign for immediate openings at a car lot. I've never did a job like that before. When I went in to give my resume, everyone looked like money, but for some reason I didn't feel intimidated. I did, however; go back to put on my best looking wig and wore the prettiest outfit I owned before officially turning in my resume. There is a book: A Boy A Burrito and A Cookie (Montañez, 2013, p.68). In it, the author explains Poor, Hunger, and Determination (PHD) all equaling wisdom. He said:

"When a person has been poor and hungry, fear disappears and in its place is a determination to get what you want." His philosophy turned him from a janitor into a C.E.O. Right before I went into that car lot, I heard a repetitive song: Go Get It (Mary Mary, 2012, track 1). Somehow; that song and Mr. Montañez philosophy added to my confidence and as God as my witness I got chosen for the job. Here I was, staying in a shelter or sleeping in my car by night, and working in an office with a view by day. When they officially took down the help wanted sign I felt myself get nervous. Perhaps it was because I was wondering how long I could hold up this facade before someone found out. Either way I was the one chosen, I was in.

Meanwhile; back at the mansion I was rapidly developing haters. One night a large family with small children was taken in. Their babies kept screaming throughout the middle of the night, so I attentively got out of my bunk bed and checked on the new arrivals. I was told that the babies might want milk and I had just brought some from the store. The other homeless women were screaming:

After College When You Don't Have A Plan

"Shut that baby up!" By me doing just the opposite, and on top of me landing a job, that sparked some jealousy. The next day I was told to come out on the front porch for a conversation. When I got out there, the owner of the mansion was sitting on the porch waiting for me. Other homeless women, whom expressed jealousy, were also outside. At first they wanted to talk about my clothes. I was 28 going on 29 years old. Just as I walked out of the first shelter and risked my own room with a bed because I was told to put on a bra, I was prepared to do the same in this situation. I was chastise for wearing shorts in the summer. When told by one of the other homeless women to take off my outfit and put something else on, I ignored her and walked out of the mansion like I was. When that conversation didn't work, they moved onto another, any excuse to kick me out. Finally; The mansion's owner ask:

"In what other ways am I being unfair to you?" Going back to our earlier conversation when I entered the porch, I pointed out that he frequently refers to me as *girl* when I am clearly a woman. That did it, next thing I knew I was packing my things, headed for the car, and never expected to return.

Unfortunately; those were the only shelters in town. I called the first shelter back; they said I was *stuck up* and that they didn't have room for me... ever. So; I found creative ways to stay clean enough to go into an office job. After work I passed by a dentist office building, adjacent to open land. I would park my car in the back of the building and sleep. When daylight came, I would use bottled water and wash in front of the open field of land. Little did I know the building had cameras attached. The next night I was awaken, not by daylight, but by a police officer's flashlight. Luckily for me he didn't give me a ticket or put me in jail, but his attitude was mean towards me and he told me to go,

Back to Tennessee part 2

so I left. After that; every evening was an on-going search after work to find the next spot to sleep. I couldn't even park on church's empty parking lot without a member driving behind me saying:

"Beat it". All of this was taking a toll on me at work in the strangest way. I was overly excited about everything, like I had ADD (Attention Deficit Disorder). It was great when I sold cars, but me sitting still long enough for the customers to finish the paper work prove to be a challenge. To compensate I became overly nice.

When I received my first pay I got hounded by Stepmom to pay her back for funding my California trip. She was hardly concern that I slept in a car, she wanted $800. This was the relationship with Stepmom. She never gave me anything without expecting it back. I; on the other hand, was in a car accident trying to wire her money I never expected back, all while I was just a college student. In fact; I didn't have parents I could go to at all for so much as a bar of soap.

Needless to say; I gave my very first check entirely to my stepmother and had nothing to show for myself. So, I moved back in with Stepmom's sister Pastor Aunt, of which I also had to pay for staying there. Things at work weren't going well. The manager was newly hired like I was, so we got along great, but the regional manager kept a close watch on me. Ever week I was reported to the manager's office for a talk on my performance. One day, the manager decided to clean house and fired the two receptionists. I didn't know what they were fired for, but as they were leaving, they looked at me as though I was a sellout. I remembered my experience working at a thrift store as a Supervisor. I gave my all to that store. I even rode a bike 6 miles on my period to open the store and they still fired me. I didn't

After College When You Don't Have A Plan

want to be told to leave so I went into my manager's office and told him I quit; which is a shame, because if I would have stayed I could have afforded my own place.

During this time I was really into my faith with God. When I received my last pay, during a time where Pastor Aunt needed $500 so her church doors wouldn't close and Stepmom called needing more money, I made a deal with God. If he got me off Pastor Aunt's couch and took care of my needs, then I would devote my entire last paycheck to helping others. Pastor Aunt paid the church rent and Stepmom got a free $60 wired to her via Western Union. All there was to do was wait for God's miracle, only it didn't come. To make matters worse Pastor Aunt moved more people into her apartment of who was not paying rent. Since my last pay check was over a week, my aunt was constantly starting fights with me. She knew I had nowhere else to go, but she wanted me out of her apartment. Where was God? I had an anxiety attack in her kitchen; lucky for me no one was there to witness it. One day, Pastor Aunt comes to me hysterical about my shoes aligned in-front of the door to the room she gave me.

"You're disrespecting my house"- she yells to me.

"By having my shoes aligned outside the door" I questioned. She saw she couldn't win that argument so she picked at something else. Finally; I snapped (yelled, screamed, and cried), packed my things in the car, and drove away from her to a nearby gas station. I had no money and nowhere to go. I called Stepdad, a couple of friends, even Stepmom whom I'd just given free money to a week ago, asking first:

"Do you trust me?" Then finally the one person that I couldn't imagine asking anything from, my sister Beatrice, she said she trusted me and wired $30. I brought $15 worth of

Back to Tennessee part 2

groceries, put the rest in the gas tank, cursed God, and headed for the next town over- Memphis.

I only had one family member who lived there, my cousin whom my sisters and I teased as a child for being too dark-skinned. I called him once I arrived. He told me he had several people living with him, so I changed the subject and ended the call politely. I sought shelters in the area, but it was different here than anywhere else I've been. Here, you had to pay by the day to get in these shelters, nothing was free. I finally found a shelter that charged $10 per day but I didn't even have that. I convinced the shelter to take me in just for the weekend free of charge. It was a Friday night. I was assigned a cot to sleep on, in an open room, shared with 20-30 other homeless women. I was to keep my belongings with me at all times because the shelter was not responsible if my things came up stolen while I slept. There were mothers with children, elderly women, young adult women, everyone except men. They slept in the next room over.

When Monday came, I packed my belongings, put on an interview outfit, and went searching for work. I drove by this big chauffeur's sign and thought: *I can do that.* So; I bagged up into a parking spot, went in, and was unknowingly filling out an application for a security guard job. The two companies were in the same building. I waited in a small room with white walls that possessed a single table with chairs. There were others in the white walled room also waiting because it was an on-the-spot interview day. I turned in my application and waited with the others until I heard my name.

"Payne!" a man's voice yelled. I quickly jumped to my feet and went into an even smaller room with white walls. Inside was a thick, older, white man, with a head full of silver hair. I complimented him; saying:

After College When You Don't Have A Plan

"Not too many men still have all their hair." He said it ran in his family. I kept the conversation on him, but eventually he got back on subject about my application. I could tell he found me charming, like one of his daughters he could never say no to. At the end of the interview he paused, then said:

"Payne, are you going to cause me pain if I decide to hire you?"

"No." I said as quickly as possible. He yelled outside the door to the receptionist named Jennifer:

"Got one more." Then turns to me and says:

"Hand in your ID and paper work to Jennifer so she can process you." He handed me a paper with directions and a schedule to attend security guard training. I jumped for joy in front of him, I couldn't believe it. I left Tara Tennessee and arrived in Memphis on Friday, then got the security guard job on Monday. I couldn't bring myself to thank God because I told myself I didn't believe in him anymore, so I looked up and thanked the cosmos. I got into my car and drove to a nearby open parking lot. Gas was running low and I had no money, so I parked the car away from view and just slept. The next day I found a public restroom and did a quick wash up, put on some clothes, and attended my very first security guard training class. The class lasted 2-3 days, then after, the company would put me to work on my first assignment.

I had a grumpy, old man that cursed a lot for an instructor. The class was in a separate adjacent building to the building I was interviewed. In class, there where desk with build-in chairs, like first grade. They were all aligned into rows. I took my seat in front of the class. Other recently hired students arrived and took their place in the front of the class too.

Back to Tennessee part 2

After the classes were over, we were given our license to be security guards. Then; we were measured and given security guard uniforms. I was then given a schedule of when I would be working and where. My car was still parked in the same spot as when I first got the job. I would walk to my classes because I didn't have money for gas. When I looked at my schedule it required me to drive many miles to my destination. So, I went next door and spoke to the receptionist, Jennifer, about my situation and she agreed to give me an advance pay for gas. She said she had never did that for someone before. I later found out that it was her own money she had given me. I promised her, when I received my first pay check, that I would give her, her money first. I now had gas money and my first assignment was securing a warehouse. I made friends with a lady working with me. She had personal problems at home and confided in me. Because I was living out of my car I tried my hardest to distance myself from her, but she knew. Once I realize she discovered my secret I left her alone completely. But it wasn't soon enough; she and I got caught talking while we were supposed to be securing the goods in the warehouse. The manager himself came to the warehouse and had a chat with me. In the end I did not lose my job, but I was transferred to another site, where I was to work alone.

Meanwhile; I was struggling to find safe places to sleep in my car after work. I would mainly park at truck stops, but gas station attendants would often call the police on me. Where ever I parked, it was never too far from my assigned post. I did this for two months until I found a small apartment on Craigslist for $275 a month.

It was spring time of 2013 when I applied for the apartment. I was greeted by a rude, over dressed, loud mouth, and

After College When You Don't Have A Plan

short property manager. She told me to come back and meet her before she went to lunch at 12 noon. I arrived at 11:30a.m and she was already on her way out the door. I was shown the apartment. It was small, but beautiful, in the heart of Midtown where all the businesses, shops, and museums were. The street the apartment was on looked upscale, a far difference from the car I was living in.

I almost turned it down because of how rude that loud mouth property manager was to me. After voicing my concerns about her to clients who rented from her, and was told she's like that with everyone, I decided to sign the lease and take the apartment. I was now out of the car, had a job that paid every week, with a brand new lease. I should have felt ecstatic, but instead I felt an overwhelming sadness brought on by rage and anger. I would come home to my new apartment just angry. Anything set me off. The apartment was remodeled inside an old house. There were six apartments inside the two story house. I was on the top floor. I remember my neighbors being afraid to speak to me because I was so angry all the time, then I would complain that no one opened up to me.

I continued this routine, work and home, until I got so fed up that I went to a psychic for directions. I still did not believe in God and I blamed him for all of my short comings. I had not been to a psychic since Corpus Christi, Texas, but her words and predictions stuck with me. She said my finances were not steady. She predicted that it will continue in this way for some time until finally I'll have a steady income. She said; it would not make me rich but it would be sufficient. Then she predicted that a past lover and I would lose interest completely. I immediately thought of that old guy who was older than both my parents. Over the years I had grown attached to him and relied on him for my **Back to**

Tennessee part 2

emotional needs. The thought of losing him was more that I could stand. Then I asked the psychic:

"Is he old?" She replied:

"No." Instead she told me that he was my age; then I thought of my old college boyfriend, but I wasn't even talking to him at the time, so I was sure it was the old guy and maybe she didn't see him right. Finally the psychic predicted that two men would come into my life: one from Africa and the other a retired military man, both young. My heart was still frightened at the possibility of losing the old guy. He had been with me throughout my entire journey, talking and encouraging me via phone conversations. I might have been physically alone throughout my journey, but that old guy picked up the phone whenever I needed a friend. So; that is why I left Corpus Christi for Tara, Tennessee.

I went to three psychics in Memphis. The first told me:

"No man is attracted to you in a way to take care of you and beware of turning into a lesbian." I snatched my $40 from her hand and left. Then; I spoke to a psychic over the phone, to test if she was for real, instead of spending my gas money driving to another failed prediction. Turns out, she too was a phony. Finally; the last psychic was closer to my house, she agreed not to take my money until I believed her predictions. When she told me I had an abortion I paid her and was all ears. She told me that I was not supposed to be in Memphis; instead she named three other states that I would most likely succeed in. One was New York. I told her I had just come from New York and how hard it was for me there. The psychic told me that things would be different if I went back. Then I asked her:

"Should I quit my job?" She said she could see I was unhappy and to quit at the beginning of the year. I ended up **After**

College When You Don't Have A Plan

quitting before New Year's and felt a familiar relief as when I quit other jobs, followed by panic when the money dwindled. I called that psychic and she told me:

"You never quit a job before landing another one." At that point I stop believing in psychics too.

By this time it was winter of 2013 and there I was: no beliefs, no job, lonely, and then my car stops. My season was turning for the worst and my only other revenue was working for temporary agencies. Although; I did get a call back from a rent-a-car service. They told me to wear khakis and polo's, and said if I was late to the interview don't bother showing up. I went into a major retail store, in a panic state and on a tight budget. The employees were slow and unconcern with my situation. I had less than two hours to buy an outfit and take a bus across town to an airport were the interview was being held. Out of frustration; I gave up, walked out of their store, and started crying. Through my tears I thought: *Wouldn't it be great to have a store specifically for interviews?* Call it: The Interview Store, everything you need for an interview you could find it at this store. I thought of; now, Duchess Kate Middleton, before she married Prince William, she used to be a buyer for retail stores. Magazines were filled with her latest fashion trends. Wouldn't it be something if I was a part of the royal family and Duchess Kate and I teamed up to launch The Interview Store. To set the store apart from the rest, we would digitize everything; from moving merchandise, usually displayed at the front of the store, to moving it towards the back, and setting computer stations in its place called *Modules*. I think this would reduce theft by 100%. At these *Modules* one would be able to take a picture of themselves and digitally try on different outfits. Much like with snap chat social media, where different images are imprinted on your photo and

Back to Tennessee part 2

some images are even movable. Plus; the idea would reduce standing at congested racks while trying on clothes that other strangers have tried on before others. Instead; there would be a comfortable chair at every *Module*. I got the idea from the movie *Clueless*, were at the beginning of the movie, Cher, played by Alicia Silverstone, tries on her school clothes, digitally placed on her computer. Plus; this new system would give designers more exposure on a computer screen rather than just a slither on a rack with other designers and discounted items. The designer, for the first year, would be no other but Gianni Versace's designs, now overseen by his sister Donatella, in honor of the people's princess, Dianna. Versace designing interview clothes would be interesting. I pictured the store's look to be sophisticated with a fire place, oak wood desk as cash registers, with personal fitters on the sales floor; like at Victoria Secret. After a purchase, a salesperson would appear from the back of the store and hand the merchandise (unworn by anyone) to the buyer. The idea is better than online shopping. I hate the wait time to receive items that get a quicker time frame receiving my payment. I wouldn't have to deal with the Police, who have two years or less of an educational background, and even less in dealing with online theft. Unfortunately; my reality kicked in. It was in all the magazines that Duchess Kate was expecting a baby. I; on the other hand, couldn't even get an interview outfit, much less an idea like this off the ground. Above all else my reality was an unemployed American who needed to survive.

Ironically; I did put in an application with the police department. When I didn't get a response right away I met Lucius. He was sitting on a stoop, near my street, next to a public car wash. I stopped in front of him and asked if he would do me a favor. He asked:

After College When You Don't Have A Plan

"What?" I told him:

"Have sex with me, I had a hard day." He smiled, got up, and kept a long distance between us as he followed me upstairs to my apartment. I had second thoughts when he entered, so I said:

"I'm sorry, I can't do this." He said:

"Okay.", and was about to put his clothes on and leave. I was so stunned by his gesture. He didn't get upset, he didn't hold me down by force like I was use to by past boyfriends, he just said okay and was going to leave me alone. Suddenly I was turned on and changed my mind again. Unfortunately; the sex was what I was use to: uncomfortable. But; he stayed with me and we talked for hours, and he smelled like fresh berries.

After that I learned he worked at the car wash near my street, he was homeless (which was odd because he smelled so good), and he was on crack. Coming from the direction of college, all I knew about drug users was what I saw on comedy television. Lucius did not resemble any of that. All his clothes were name brand; including his shoes, he kept good hygiene; except for his teeth and he was muscular. Most crack addicts that I saw on television were skinny and dirty. That old guy in Tara stopped talking to me, he moved on with a new lady. I had not made any friends in Memphis due to my financial hardship. Why not Lucius? I thought. I moved him in with me and he didn't last seven days before feigning for drugs and picking fights with me to get to them. When he left I didn't let him back in, then a whole six months went by before I heard from him. He went away to Nashville and met someone, then called to throw it in my face. While left alone; I fantasied, as I often did when reality backed me into a corner, about my life as a royal: What would royalty do? Keep it moving? I started going downtown where tourists

Back to Tennessee part 2

were and teamed up with blues musicians to sing as a contestant. It was a great distraction. My first solo was by Billy Holiday: God bless the child. I didn't even know the words, I sang along to lyrics on a paper I printed out at the library. I did okay; some even gave a tip in the basket for my performance. After though; while singing other songs, it became a downward slope of humiliation, so I stopped going back. On the back of that printed-out-paper I kept, I wrote how I would meet Prince Harry. Ironically; he and his brother William came to Memphis. I took it as a sign that someday; despite all that happened, I would end up in their family.

Meanwhile; the police academy called me in for training, only to run out of city funds, and so I was not hired. I didn't give up, but instead pursued to take the Law School Admissions Test (LSAT) to go back to school and become a lawyer. I could not afford the test but financial assistance was available. Because I qualified, I was eligible to take an expensive test up to 3 times for free. I studied hard, only to have the location change to take the test at the last minute. I couldn't find the location in time, and it would be another 6 months to retake it. Luckily; I found comfort in my next door neighbor. He loved my thighs and I liked his accent, he was short but sexy. I knew it was wrong and dangerous; if we broke up he would be next door to me until one of us moved out. Ironically; that's exactly what happened. Also; I couldn't find regular employment. The temporary service jobs stop calling me in for daily work; so I went on unemployment, but unemployment ran out. I had no car to get around and although I told myself I didn't believe in psychics or in anything anymore, I kept in mind what the psychic said about me not supposed to be in Tennessee. When I got my last unemployment check, I sold everything I had in my apartment and brought a Greyhound ticket as far as my money could get me which was

After College When You Don't Have A Plan

Atlanta, GA, one of the states the psychic mention I was supposed to be in to be successful. I was miserable in Atlanta. I waited in a bus station for four days. Most times; because I didn't have a ticket going anywhere, they made me wait out in the street like a homeless person. I called everyone I knew asking for money to get me the rest of the way to New York. They all teased saying I shouldn't have left my apartment in Memphis with nowhere to go. But I couldn't pay my rent. I would have been homeless on the street and car-less in Memphis otherwise.

One day I was sitting outside on a curb, wondering how I was going to come up with the money to get to New York. I had even sold all of my food stamps to the Greyhound manager and that still wasn't enough to get me a ticket going to New York. During that time it was the 4th of July weekend of 2014 and the tickets were more expensive. A man came up to me as I was on the curb, outside, and told me that I'm asking for what I want the wrong way. He told me that I shouldn't ask for a specific amount of money, but instead ask for help on the ticket. He told me there was a Nun who gave sermons in the park and to ask her for help in the way we discussed. It worked. Although; I'm not sure why, she was constantly surrounded by needy people. Who was I that she paid $164.89 for a one-way ticket for me to get to New York? I was still very much angry at God and refused to acknowledge his existence, so I was left with no one to thank but the universe. Thanks.

Back to Tennessee part 2

COMMENTS

Leave a comment...

Vicky127

Really?

John1294

I knew it! Didn't I say she should have stayed in New York?

> Suzanne Merriweather
>
>
>
> John1294 At this point I don't care where she stays as long as she stays still.

After College When You Don't Have A Plan

BigPaul

Suzanne Merriweather Amen!

Miketheman

Suzanne Merriweather I second that.

Lacy Hamilton

What happened to that Interview Store idea? Just because Duchess Kate has kids doesn't mean she can't put this on her to-do agenda once her life gets on the right track.

Big Paul

So she left Corpus Christi, Texas for the old guy? Why was she even worried about losing anybody? They all have a roof over their heads. That was the time to be selfish and just worry about herself because nobody else was doing it, including the old guy.

Back to Tennessee part 2

Miketheman

BigPaul I agree. You can't give what you don't have including your time.

Elizabeth Rochelle FeelJoy

How is the lesson process going? Hope your learning what not to do. Read on to see if there is a wrap to all this madness.

NEW YORK AGAIN

Chapter 7
New York again

It was the summer of 2014 when I arrived and went back to the same shelter, which use to be a school, but looked like a prison. Ms. Rowe and Smith no longer worked there, but the director of the shelter, Ms. Crite, was still there and recognized me instantly. Things had changed since I was there five years prior. This time staff did not address the homeless by their bed numbers (as if we were in jail), we were addressed by our names. Also; before, the shelter could not just kick you out, but instead have you transferred to someplace else. This time the rules had changed; now the shelter could put you out on the street up to 40 days, and no other shelter was allowed to take you in during that time. Even the numbers on the beds had changed to letters. Maybe it was my complaint to the mayor's office years ago that did the trick, but I was not in old New York anymore.

Unfortunately; the wait time to be seen by an intake specialist, so that I can be assigned a bed, had changed to a longer wait. Once assigned a bed, I had gone through the motions of registering, I was a New Yorker all over again. I got assigned a male case manager this time around. He was the go-to-guy when you needed an easy-going person who would approve anything. Unfortunately; he was also what I call a *burned out* case manager. He saw his job as pointless and rarely showed up for work. I called him out on it. He said:

New York Again

"Why should I give my all for you guys who sit outside the building on a curb all day; I help those who help themselves." I had a thought: *If he only helped those who helped themselves, then what did we need him for*? Right then and there I reminded him and said:

"Who are you talking about, "You guys?", have you ever seen me out there on the curb? And even so; aren't those the ones who need help the most?" I ran out of his office in tears because he was where I wanted to be: a job and not in a shelter starting from scratch at 30 years old, and there he was throwing it in my face,

"I help those who help themselves." It seemed all staff working there were like that. They would show up to work wearing the best and the latest outfits just to show-up us homeless people. Every work day was a fashion show. Their demeanor's spoke volumes: Better than you, always will be. Even the cooks were snobbish.

Days after that incident I got my first job in New York City. I had my own cubical and worked in an office conducting surveys over the phone as a Survey Representative. Ironically; it was the same job I turned down 5 years earlier to move to Chicago and live with Stepmom. It was the type of job that hired anybody as long as they could read, and I was grateful for it. Meanwhile; back at the shelter, I urged Ms. Crite, the shelter director, to change my case manager. When she was unwilling I went over her department head, they phoned her, and next thing I knew I had a new case manager and was sent to a different shelter. This shelter was less crowded, rules more relaxed, and in a better neighborhood. Here; I was able to get on a budget plan to save up for my own apartment. It was an all single women's shelter for workers only. I guess gratefulness was replaced with a

After College When You Don't Have A Plan

more arrogant personality type because the women had jobs. That is the vibe I got from the women in the new shelter. There was one woman in particular who worked as a hairdresser. She was big, stocky, and always carried an angry look on her face. This woman constantly picked on and harassed another woman who was much smaller. She washed her hands a lot and said nothing to defend herself against the hostile hairdresser. I spoke up in her defense every now and then, but even the hairdresser intimidated me at times. It was the saddest day once the timid woman spoke and told me her story. She just had a baby, and in the hospital her baby was taken away by social services because she lived in a shelter. She went back and forth to court to try to gain custody of her 4 month old child. One could just look at her and tell that the ordeal was taking a toll on her. But, that's the thing, everybody has a story. I wondered; if that hairdresser had known the timid woman's story, would she have treated her differently?

I had bullies of my own. I made an oath at the time that I did not believe in God, that people decided their own fates. Others in that shelter did not feel the same way, so I was constantly bullied as a result. During all of this I had decided to do the impossible and take the Law School Admissions Test (LSAT) again. When I lived in Memphis one of my male friends gave me some valuable advice on bullies. He said:

"You got to check them when the incident first happens, otherwise they'll come back with even more people to bully you." I had no problem standing up for myself against men, but because of the authoritative relationship I had with Stepmom growing up, psychologically, women were harder for me to stand up to. I had just taken the LSAT and failed it with a low score of 140. Things got so hostile that I had my first fight. I was involved in a fist fight that put me in the hospital for a dislocated shoulder. After

New York Again

that incident though, it cured me from any psychological and sexist view I had toward physical confrontations.

Shortly after, Stepmom called from South Chicago and told me that my brother Theodore was in the hospital. He had two or three open heart surgeries back-to-back. I thought he was going to die while I was stuck in the New York shelters, fighting over nonsense. I took the money I saved, and without question, packed up what little I had, and took a one-way bus to South Chicago. Theodore was unrecognizable when I arrived at the hospital. His whole body was puffy from the surgeries. He recognized me though and allowed me to hug and kiss him. I stayed for two days before Stepmom started to get on my nerves and I on hers. I flew back this time to New York. Fortunately; my job was still waiting for me, but my shelter wasn't. I arrived at two o' clock in the afternoon and had to wait until the 10p.m curfew to see if someone missed their bed so I could claim it. When everyone showed up I had to wait again, out in the lobby, on a hard fold-up-chair, and sitting up. I was already tired from the plane ride, only to wait until a bed became available was murder. I had a couple of hundred dollars left. I took a chance and paid a $200 non-refundable fee to an agency to find me a room-for-rent. I was placed on 131st street near NYU. I had to pay $150 to the renter for a deposit and another $150 for the rent. Rent was due every week, but I was out of the shelter. For the first time I saw the city at night pass the 10p.m curfew and it was beautiful.

I made a friend in the shelter, she also left the shelter and stayed with her mom on 170th street. I went out to a club for the first time with she and her mom and enjoyed the night life New York had to offer. Unfortunately; renting a room in a stranger's apartment caused tension. The apartment owner was a little-old-woman that traveled a lot and left the management of her

After College When You Don't Have A Plan

apartment to her wild and rebellious daughter with a smart mouth. Her daughter called me *country* when I complained of bed buds:

"You from the country you should be used to it." She even asked me for the rent early so that she can go clubbing. Enough was enough, so I moved in with my friend and her mother, paying only $125 per week.

During this time it was after Christmas 2014, and my job was experiencing some cut backs but I still remained working there. My hours at work was reduced so much that I had to file for unemployment. Meanwhile; I didn't have enough to cover the rent each week. I tried working for a temp service again, but they were experiencing lack of work as well. I quietly moved out of my friend's and her mom's room-for-rent and tried to go back into the shelter. Though; by the time I got there it was over crowded still, so I was taken on a bus to a shelter in the Bronx. I was in tears because I had come so far only to go backwards. This shelter was full of older woman with disabilities. My room was shared only with one other roommate as oppose to 10 other women or more. I still worked at my job. While there I met a guy who kept me laughing rather than crying. He took me to Starbucks but cried *broke* at the checkout. It was becoming a routine so much so that I yelled at him outside a restaurant, walked off, and never saw him again. After that I got deeply depressed, thinking I was all by myself, alone, and no one cared about me. So; I turned to cigarettes for the first time in my life. They were cheap, 50 cents a stick, and it felt good to blow all my problems in a cloud of smoke to the wind. I got addicted instantly, even now, I want one. I also started drinking, but that made me happy not sad, as I discovered I am a happy drunk. I blamed God so much so that I quit believing in his existence completely. Along the way I met a 60-old-young-spirit named

New York Again

Edna. She and her family were born in England, but her accent was no different than the classic New Yorker. She reminded me to have fun in my circumstances. Sure; I was in the shelter, but I also didn't have any bills or financial responsibilities. I was saving up all my money at that time with nothing to show for it. It took me 5 months to save up $1200 when Stepmom called from, South Chicago, and told me that my brother was in the hospital. Only to heighten the situation by telling me that it might be my last chance to see him. So; of course I blew just about all the $1200 I saved up to get my own apartment, and took a pause on shelter life to be with my brother. I took a Greyhound all the way to the suburbs of South Chicago just to see him. My brother is autistic, so none of my efforts meant anything to him, let alone is remembered. Stepmom and I were arguing on what the best care for him would be. I was insistent, that it was not to be smothered in her care. My brother would sit around the house and only get up to eat, I blamed her for his condition of being so overweight that he needed a double heart surgery. Stepmom would leave my brothers and sisters inside the house and take the keys with her. Sometimes she'll be gone the entire day. They were not to leave the house without Stepmom's permission and she never gave them that permission. Mostly; all of my siblings that still live with her receive some type of disability check. Stepmom does not work, so you do the math. For as long as I can remember we lived in houses, in fancy neighborhoods, and got evicted. Stepmom would constantly buy things we couldn't afford. There was no one to stand up to her and tell her no or to stop. She divorced Stepdad and her latest husband, Dean, was a push over, and so she did things her way while the family paid for it. It is not my intent to put her down as a Stepmom but instead reveal circumstances that may help someone going through the same thing. It is difficult to react when it comes to any parent. Stepmom attended every

After College When You Don't Have A Plan

parent conference meeting when I was growing up, she was the only one to fight for me when teachers picked on me or tried to place me in special ed classes, and when we were evicted, having to stay in a shelter sometimes, she was there even when Stepdad's moved on. So; it's hard to write her up as the villain, but contrary to write her up as a saint.

After I had seen my brother, it was apparent that Stepmom was going to kick me out again. After a day and a half I was no longer newly arrived and she wanted me out and I wanted to get out. So; now, that was more money I was going to be out of returning to New York. I arrived 2 o'clock in the afternoon and had to sit out in their lobby until 10 o'clock p.m., waiting until someone missed their curfew so I could get their bed. By this time I had not slept or rested for a total of 12 hours. I took my last $500 to rent a room from a small agency called Rent-a-room, they required a $200 nonrefundable fee to view their listings, $150 deposit once a listing was found, plus $150 rent to move in. That was all my money, plus I had to repeat $150 every week after that. After the holiday's I lost my job working as a Survey Representative, business slowed down so I was back at the shelters.

I took advantage of the situation of moving back into the shelter system and saved money working odd jobs to go to City Court and change my name. I figured Elizabeth Ann Payne was irony destine for a miserable life, so I officially changed it to Elizabeth Rochelle FeelJoy. I kept Elizabeth because everybody knew me by that name and I didn't want to confuse anyone. I ditched the adjunct "Ann" and replaced it with Rochelle from the Character "Everybody Hates Chris". I wanted a name that was not going to make me a push over, but instead a name people took seriously and were afraid of.

New York Again

At the time, when I was transferred to another shelter with mostly senior citizens, who were about that thug life style, they would pick fights with me and anyone else they thought was weak. Somehow; after the name change, I think it did transform me into this alternate personality. Instead of staying low when someone disrespected me, I met the challenge head on, and I became the one bullies were afraid to step to.

I played with the idea of all sorts of last names, but FeelJoy (the F and J are capitalized) one day just popped in my head. Ideally; this made sense to go from Payne to FeelJoy, plus no one in the universe carried the name, and the name was not associated with slavery. So; on January 2015, I decided to be the new and improved: Elizabeth Rochelle FeelJoy. A name fit for a royal. The royal Princes themselves don't even carry an official surname. That is one of the many reasons I liked the idea of being in the royal family, I would get to keep my name. If Prince Harry and I were to have a little girl I would name her Sweet, Sweet FeelJoy (no middle name). If it was a boy, I would hold onto the name I had been carrying around ever since college: Tommy-Tyrone (with the hyphen), so it would be Tommy-Tyrone FeelJoy. It sounds like a name one can depend on, a strong name. One could always rely on a Tommy-Tyrone. For some reason, if Prince Harry and I didn't have little Sweet, Tommy-Tyrone, or each other, then I wouldn't give those names to anyone. I only hoped for a Sweet FeelJoy and a Tommy-Tyrone with Harry and me.

My friend Edna was right, have fun in your circumstances. If I was going to spend money, spend it on myself so I could at least see where the money went. Another thing I learned from Edna is God is real; the test of my faith is when I'm going through. Together we went to museums we couldn't afford,

After College When You Don't Have A Plan

but it was free on the first of the month. We went to expensive restaurants on paydays; our favorite was Dallas BBQ's. We even went to the Oscars together, hosted by a bar on the Upper East Side. She taught me to enjoy my life instead of complain about it. Edna found a beautiful basement rental and like a true friend she let me stay with her until I got on my feet. During that time, I got a job working from home, selling education to the unemployed. Ironically; I went to college without a plan, racked up tuition bills I still haven't attempted to pay off, and here I was selling college as a means to survive. But; I was in the perfect position mobility wise. I no longer had to stay in New York job bound; I was free to live places that were cheap while making New York pay. So; when Edna complained that her landlord did not want me staying with her, guest or otherwise, and I was given the ultimatum to leave by the time she came home from work, I could at least say I had a job.

Also; I had given up on the LSAT exam and becoming a lawyer. I would often go to a career center where one can print resume's and use the computers for free. One day, this guy over hears me say that I'm studying for the LSAT. He mentioned that he not only took the test and passed, but that he is a lawyer. Excited; I asked if he would help me study. He agreed and sometime after we met up and he told me about himself. He revealed that he was in a shelter and that it was hard to find work in the big city of New York. Law is essentially sales and advertisement of being the best at counsel before a Judge in a U.S court of law. I got into law because I defended myself in court against a motel for withholding my money after checking out of an unclean room rented to me. I won my case, even against the defendant's expensive lawyer. I made the decision that I would never need a lawyer, but instead become one. Unfortunately; more and more people think this way as well, there by, only the

New York Again

the most heard of lawyers are hired instead. Needless-to-say, I no longer had an interest in pursuing law. It's embarrassing to end up in a shelter with a Bachelor's degree, but even more so with a higher education.

COMMENTS

Leave a comment...

Jackie1workaholic

Well; at least now there is a job that travels with her. I just hope that she can hold onto it.

After College When You Don't Have A Plan

Miketheman

Jackie1workaholic oh God yes! After the way this story has been going I'll take anything positive.

BigPaul

Jackie1workaholic If she holds onto this job she could save up towards a house. That way she won't have to keep moving.

Suzanne Merriweather

I like the name Sweet FeelJoy, but doubt names has any influence on the outcome of one's life.

BigPaul

She shouldn't have spent that money she worked so hard to save. If she would have continued saving she could have landed an apartment.

New York Again

Lacy Hamilton

BigPaul But her brother could have died in the hospital.

Elizabeth Rochelle FeelJoy

So what happens next?

FLORIDA

After College When You Don't Have A Plan

Chapter 8

Florida

I left Edna's and moved to Florida in 2015. I rented a room from a white man named Richard. He lived in a house with a pool, in the middle of Florida, in a town called: Clewiston. He had a live in black girlfriend more than half his age with two kids they made together, and she was pregnant with another on the way. I paid $125 a week and I lasted until $1125 was paid, the equivalent of 3 months.

During this time I was the victim of pregnancy rage. I did not have a spouse of my own like other room renters. Instead, I came there by myself with a job, and no kids. The girlfriend hated me and was always suspicious. In fact; I had the whole town talking and wondering who I was. Richard; my room lord, made an art of saving a dollar where ever he could. He was obsessed with money. One day we got to know each other. On and off I was still smoking cigarettes, while Richard and his pregnant girlfriend enjoyed weed. Richard asked:

"What is most important in this world?" My response was love, his was money. He told me a story of how he witnessed his friend's father suicide after losing his job. He said:

"That man had been working for a company half of his life until one day they decided to let him go." As a boy Richard decided right then and there that: 1. Money mattered, 2. He'll work for nobody but himself, and 3. He would lie, cheat, or steal

Florida

to get what he wanted. He told me he took the identity of a dead person to collect unemployment. I thought; *where did I go wrong?* I lived my life trying to do the right things: finishing college, earn money legally, and here I was a renter and Richard was the landlord. In my defense I argued love. To get *things* are all well in good, but love gives those things collected purpose and meaning. Afterwards; he determined I wasn't black but confused, and continued collecting my weekly rent.

One night his girlfriend went into labor. Conveniently when Richard went out of town and didn't answer her calls. He took one of the kids with him, but left the other. When she went into labor I got a call in the middle of the night from Richard, asking me to watch their child while his girlfriend went to the hospital to give birth. There were other "renters" renting rooms in the house, but I was asked. I thought; since doing this, Richard wasn't going to charge me rent for that week, so I agreed. I was so wrong, he not only still expected me to pay while I miss going online working to babysit his child, but; me doing that enabled him to make his money on the road, and in return I got nothing to show for my generosity. Nobody cared. It was just expected that I do more.

Meanwhile; tension was building up. The couple renting a room next to me was physically fighting, Richard hired a house keeper and was paying her in free room and board which pissed me off because I was already cleaning around the house, tending to his kids, and he still charged me $125 per week. The girlfriend was back from the hospital, angry at me because I refused to get involved when she and Richard trash talked of each other to me, *just-a-renter*. I knew they were going to get back together, so I stayed out of it.

After College When You Don't Have A Plan

During this time, I had been talking to my ex again, George. He still lived in Chicago while I tried to make the best of things in Florida. He told me his regrets of not stepping up about the baby we made. He said:

"I assumed you were lying to me again, just like in college. You had me go with you to a clinic knowing you weren't pregnant. When you told me you were pregnant again, I thought you were lying to get me to pay your rent." I Facebooked George, because he didn't have a phone of his own during those times, about the time and location on where the abortion would be taken place. He had gotten into the military so I meant nothing to him when he financially found his way. Somehow; I was convinced that he was sorry, that it was all a big misunderstanding, and to give us another chance. The military was not what he thought it would be and at that time, little did I know, he was broke again. We were supposed to move in with each other at his apartment, but he revealed himself as always. He told me earlier on, when I still lived in New York; his rent was only $100 per month. He was given housing for military veterans. Apparently; he forgot that conversation, because he was now asking me for $100 per month to move in with him, saying we'll go 50/50. Then and there I stopped talking to the guy who once asked me for a naked picture of myself using someone else phone.

And; in the house I rented a room in, I felt trapped. When I would go to the laundry room; the girlfriend was there, when I would go into the kitchen; she was there, when I would go outside for a smoke; she would be there. And, what was worse is she teamed up with the housekeeper Richard hired to bully me. I was paying $125 per week, faithfully, to be bullied by a 22 year old mom with now 3 kids. I was living in a state I had never been to before, and I lived out in the middle of nowhere. There was a

Florida

bus but it stopped running after 5p.m. I was in no position to pack my things and run like I was used to. I cornered the girlfriend in the kitchen and demanded that we talk about the situation. Being young, she only wanted to fist fight, but there were small children present and I was too grown, 32, to stoop down to her level. Once I got her talking she said what I already suspected.

"I never liked you and it was not my idea to have you watch our child in the first place, that was Richard's idea, we made a mistake with you." As she said the words, it was as though a bullet had hit me dead on in my heart, and I fought back the tears. True; I did not have to accept watching their child when Richard called me in the middle of the night, I did not have to feed, bathe, or watch their child for the entire day. Instead; I could have flat-out-told-him no, worked my job, and made money for that day. Not exhaust myself cleaning their entire house when he hired a lazy, weed smoking, housekeeper for that. I just had to feel wanted, a part of a family, a team player, and it got me nowhere.

Richard was standing right beside her and said nothing to the contrary. All I could get out was: "I paid over a thousand dollars living here and this is the thanks I get?" She said:

"Thanks for the money" like making a joke of the matter. I turned directly to Richard and said:

"I'm giving you my weeks' notice on moving out and I want my deposit of $125 back." A couple of days later the girlfriend and her kids moved out, while Richard tried to convenience me to stay. My mind was made up and on the day of my departure he had already moved in yet another young girl he had gotten pregnant, but I moved out went back home to the state of Tennessee.

After College When You Don't Have A Plan

COMMENTS

Leave a comment...

Miketheman

If I wasn't so upset from all the let downs of the previous chapters, I would feel sympathy for her in this chapter. At lease she still has her job. She still has her job-right?

Vicky127

So; she keeps finding inventive ways to her living situations, how long can she keep this up? She's over 30-years-old.

Florida

BigPaul

All this money she's paid out could have went towards something of her own.

> Suzanne Merriweather
>
>
>
> BigPaul How? Being a home owner takes the right frame of mind. She's all over the place just trying to survive. And all this with a Bachelor's degree. SMH.

> Miketheman
>
>
>
> Suzanne Merriweather Maybe it takes more than just a degree. If she knew her home-life was as dysfunctional as we just read then she should have set aside some of that school money towards a down payment on a house. As far as the jobs, throughout this whole process she's landed some pretty decent jobs because she has her degree.

TENNESSEE; BLOOM WHERE YOU ARE PLANTED

After College When You Don't Have A Plan

Chapter 9

Tennessee; bloom where you are planted

When I arrived in Memphis I already had plans for a rental room waiting for me. The room was not attractive and my neighbors; an older black couple, were loud alcoholics. I needed reinforcements so that I wouldn't get pushed around like in Florida, so; I sought after Lucius, the ex-boyfriend who smoked crack. Sure; I left him behind because he had a drug problem, but he was strong and precisely what I needed to get my point across. Although; he was someone to watch out for as well.

Earlier on, after Lucius and I broke up, and he left me to move to a new city, he would call me from time to time. Then, have some woman call from an unlisted number, telling me to leave her man alone. Yea; Lucius was that guy. He eventually came back to Memphis, claimed he got awarded disability, and could take care of me. Lucius never had a job, instead he had a hustle at a car wash; that or begging strangers for money. I swear he did not present himself in that way when I met him. So; when he asked to get back together with me and I turned him down; I instead demanded that he pay me back the money he borrowed from me, which was $129. We went back and forth on this, until finally I threaten to turn him into social security for using his social security checks to buy drugs. He turned the tables on me and filed for a restraining order...and won his case! I had to pay over $200 for an appeal. I got the restraining order reversed and had not seen a dime of my money since.

Tennessee; bloom where you are planted

Now; present day, I've sought Lucius out and he now lived with me in my rented room. The agreement was that he pays me $10 per day while I kept up with the weekly rent of $100. I still had my work from home job as a career counselor, so I honestly thought this set up would work. Unfortunately; in November 2015, the unthinkable happened, that, up until this point, I had been able to avoid my whole life: He hit me. That bastard turned on me. I got him to live with me to protect me and instead I needed protection from him. And who was there to protect me? My noisy alcoholic neighbors: ironic.

I knew I needed to leave Memphis; in fact I should have skipped that city altogether and moved back to Tara where I could have saved up my money but I was stubborn. After that incident with Lucius, it took a drug collector barging into my room unannounced, asking have I seen another neighbor of mine that had moved out because he owed money for drugs. There was not a stubborn bone in my body after that. I took the next Greyhound going out and moved back in with Pastor Aunt in Tara, Tennessee.

A full circle twice and it landed me in Tara, Tennessee on the first of the year of 2016. The good news was that I was still employed working from home. The bad news was that I was living with Pastor Aunt again, where any money I made became hers. All over again it was paying for: the attendance to church functions, tithes and offerings, rent and utilities, and an endlessness parade of just paying her.

Meanwhile; I could not afford to move out and I was stuck. She mentioned income based housing apartments were taking applications for new tenants. All that was required with my application was my birth certificate and by that time my new name was already on it. From then on my name had officially

After College When You Don't Have A Plan

become Elizabeth Rochelle FeelJoy; with the "J" capitalized and all one word. Sometime after, I gave God a vow. I was sick of the merry-go-round I put myself in, back and forth from New York to Tennessee with other states in between. During that time, I was smoking a half a pack of cigarettes per day. I had already been to the hospital on Valentine's Day for heart irregularity, but I kept on smoking. So; I made a bargain with God: I would give up cigarettes and only have sex again with my husband; in fact, not even allow a man to kiss me until I married, in exchange that God takes care of me. Cold turkey I gave up cigarettes and sex then and there. Four months went by, just as I was about to have a nervous breakdown in Pastor Aunt's kitchen because I couldn't stand living with her any longer, I got the call for an apartment. I paid no upfront costs, plus received assistance on my utilities every month. Then; the local television news station called and hired me working the cameras. And to sweeten the deal I was able to buy myself a car.

Then the test in my new found faith in God starts to set in. By now, I was a full member at Pastor Aunt's church again. A strain developed at my new job working at the news station. Somehow, I had developed stupid and couldn't follow simple task, like operating a camera. If I did not wise up and get smart soon, I was going to lose my job. On top of that, the lead news anchor discovered that I didn't know what I was doing behind the cameras, and exposed me like she was chasing a hot story. No one would follow my directions on set, disrespect was mounting, and then I got the call:

"Don't come in you're fired." I must say I was relieved. I still had my other job and a new apartment. One of my many dream jobs, working at a news station, had become more stressful than it was worth. I felt better and calmer leaving it.

Tennessee; bloom where you are planted

On top of that my car started to act up. I was sharing it with Pastor Aunt. Next thing I knew my car completely broke down after a midnight run to Walmart. I called my aunt, although I knew she did not have a car, but she let my uncle stay with her who did have a car.

"I'm stranded at a closed gas station" I told her.

"I'll pray for you" she said and hung up the phone, probably went back to sleep. So I called her back and asked her to have my uncle pick me up and drive me back home. She said no, and hung up again, and went back to sleep; probably. I couldn't believe it. I put her above my own stepmother. She and my stepmother has had this ongoing feud for as long as I'd been born. In my adult years I have resisted my stepmother and attached myself to her arch enemy: Pastor Aunt. Both have manipulated me out of finances, but I always returned back to Pastor Aunt, and now this happens. I let her use my car when she didn't have one, and when I got strained at a closed gas station, at 4 o'clock in the morning, she wouldn't even ask my uncle to help me.

After staying up all night until the next morning, outside, in the cold, and near the broken down car, a surprised help from a stranger came along. She bumped my car with hers all the way back to the parking lot of my apartment. I called for repairs and left Pastor Aunt completely alone after that. I went to Meineke, my go to for all my car repairs. Their located everywhere; they were like my automotive family. I had been going to them ever since college, a total of 11 years. They had it towed to their shop, awaiting an estimate. Disastrously; with this particular shop, I was told one thing and given another. This deception costs me over $3000 for a car worth $600. It was now toward December of 2016 and my work-from-home job sent me an email saying their

After College When You Don't Have A Plan

letting me go. Here I was; in debt, unemployed, and broke, in an unfurnished apartment.

During this time, back in Chicago, Stepmom lost yet another house. She was homeless with my four younger siblings, all over the age 18; she raised them to rely on her heavily. I still lived in Tennessee and I had 2 other sisters, closer in age, which still lived in Chicago. None of them could help. We were all struggling in our own way. The situation sent my sister, Samantha, on a suicide scare because she said all the pressure to rescue our stepmom, just because she lived in Chicago, was too much for her to deal with. I called the Police in Chicago from Tennessee when Samantha text me she was going to end her life. In doing that; Samantha and I stop talking, she no longer took my calls. Though; after that incident, no one expected anything from Samantha again. I really needed Samantha and all my family for sound advice, after all; it takes a scammer to know one. I had just gotten scammed by Meineke, took out a loan I shouldn't have to pay for car repairs that led to the scam, and worst yet I just lost my work-from-home job. Everything started crashing down in December of 2016, just in time for the New Year.

I went to court to prove: Breach of Verbal Contract against Meineke, for promising me a low mileage motor, only to switch it with a motor with double the miles, of which they forced me to pay for in advance. Before the case, I had not driven or had access to my car since Meineke had it towed off my lot in August of 2016. They refused to give it back to me when I refused to pay the $500 remaining balance on now double the miles. So; for 3 months I had to walk in rain, snow, sleet, or catch the bus, all while paying on a loan for a car I no longer had access to. Since my way around town was limited, I had no one to talk to. Ex-Boyfriends would come over, just to leave when I refuse to sleep

Tennessee; bloom where you are planted

with them for a ride. My faith with God was shaky yet steady. Earlier in that year I had promised God that I would not sleep with a man or so much as let a guy kiss me unless he was my husband and that I would not smoke cigarettes. Tony was one of the best sex of my life and I turned him away because of that promise made. I was left with an almost empty apartment; except for a dining room table set I managed to buy before my jobs ended. Also; a queen size airbed and a small futon in the living room, not even close to what I had planned for my new apartment. I no longer had the job at the local television-news-station, no work-from-home job, no car, no boyfriends, and no family. It was just me, God, and that promise I made.

    I went to court and lost. I was ordered to pay what was due in return for the possession of my car. I couldn't afford to appeal the case, so I was left with: Court costs (over $200), A loan that paid for that double-the-miles engine put in (over $2500), credit card used to get the car back (over $500), along with my day-to-day bills. Once again I thought of the royals; If I had any shot of becoming one, despite all that happened to me, I couldn't allow my precious name to be associated with any discrepancies, even when my name was *Payne*. It still represented me. That's why, just like the restraining order put on me by Lucius, I fought back and appealed. Only; I couldn't afford to do the same in this situation, so I went out and got the first available job offer at a retirement home as a Resident Assistant. I was basically a servant. I did everything from bathing a senior to hand feeding them just to pay off my debt. It took me 2 months into the job to finally get rid of that loan. I gave all my pay, even my income tax money at the beginning of 2017, to be able to walk into their office, slap the money on their desk, and walk out like a boss. It felt amazing.

After College When You Don't Have A Plan

Since my failed court case with Meineke I've also learned to forgive. Back in grade school and during recess, my sisters and I would go to a girl's house in my class. She didn't have any friends outside of my sisters and me. Her family was Jehovah Witnesses and although I didn't know what that meant at the time, I did know it separated this girl from the other kids. My sister's and I were brought up Apostolic and we had to wear skirts and dresses all the time when all the other kids wore pants, so we could relate. Her mom would feed us little square ham sandwiches, cookies, and orange Kool-Aid. Then; one day during school, we were all called to the Principal's office. Her mom, our stepmom, other people, including my sister's and I were there. Her mom told our stepmom that we came over to her house often. Stepmom called her a liar much like the judge told me in the case against Meineke. Also; just like in that case, the mother turned to me, like I had turned towards the store owner, looking for this person to own up to the truth, and like me back then, the store owner kept silent and turned away from me. I was more afraid of what Stepmom would do to me than coming clean so that Stepmom would stop chanting liar at that mother. Maybe Meineke was under the same pressure, that the store owner would rather hear the judge falsely accuse me of being a liar rather than speak up and tell the truth, and so I forgave Meineke.

Things started to look up. I became unavailable because I worked so much, so everybody wanted me around again. I even got a call from that old guy, but I didn't answer, and that felt amazing. The job, however; became a strain. Injuries were happening to me at work; like, injuring my back picking up a resident, being bit all over my body by something in the residence's room, or being called to the office for ridiculous things like: You're too bossy. Times like these made me miss working from home away from people and germs. The last straw

Tennessee; bloom where you are planted

came when I got punched in the face by an Alzheimer's resident. I knew she couldn't help it, but that whole incident was over looked by my employers and I was even ordered to remain working. On top of that; I had to deal with a nurse trying to use her position to make an example out of me. So; I went home and scrubbed myself clean as it had become my routine to do after every shift. Then I wrote a departure email to my employer. I turned in my badge and uniform the next day. Just like that I was free and unemployed. Not what I wanted to associate my new name with: Unemployed...again and again.

    Also; I took the opportunity to use the job's medical insurance upon quitting. I was told my insurance stopped abruptly on the date of my departure, so I had to pay hundreds out-of-pocket. My experience of it all at the doctor's office was even worse. The staff wouldn't even take me to the side. Instead; they blasted my business for the entire lobby to hear. I couldn't pay all at once, so my doctor withheld my results until I paid in full. During examination my privacy was invaded. My doctor did my exam and tried to discuss my results with, what he calls: A scribe. She was basically shadowing his job. She had no medical license. When I asked her to leave, my doctor raised his voice at me, demanding that I repeat myself. On her way out, my doctor insured her that he'll fill her in on our discussion.

    I don't know if doctors are paid more to diagnose a patient as HPV positive, but during the examination he seemed insistent on testing me for it, even though I lied and told him I never had a history of STD's. After the unprofessional way he presented himself, I lied to see if he'll tell me if something was wrong despite payment. He didn't. The payment mattered. Months later; when I was finally able to pay in full, the doctor told me I had a normal Pap smear; although, I also tested positive for HPV again.

College When You Don't Have A Plan

I could have passed what I had along to someone, including his family due to his negligence of information. He didn't care, but I did. Thankfully; I kept my promise to God and refused to have sex, or so much as let a guy kiss me, until I'm married. I don't have symptoms and I hadn't had sex since 2015, even then I used protection. I got a second opinion from another doctor who had more values. After looking at my results from the previous Doctor, the new Doctor explained, that having HPV with the After results of a normal Pap smear is a good sign that someday the virus will go away on its own. I will continue to monitor my situation; in the mean time I celebrate a normal exam.

COMMENTS

Leave a comment...

John1294

She stopped dating-good. She needs to take some much needed time for her.

Tennessee; bloom where you are planted

Vicky127

John1294 I agree. She also stopped smoking, good. I didn't like reading that flaw about her.

Lacy Hamilton

Vicky127 I hope her next move is that Interview Store she talked about opening with Duchess Kate Middleton in Chapter 6. That was a good idea. At least then she'll work for herself and her money will truly be hers.

College When You Don't Have A Plan

Vicky127

Lacy Hamilton Be realistic! She's in no position to work for herself. That takes planning, skills she lacks. I think the discipline of working for someone would do her some good.

Suzanne Merriweather

It seemed everything was going good; two jobs, a car, and she moved out of Pastor Aunt's place. Now everything is taking a nose dive again? But we're almost towards the end. Where's the happy ending?

Elizabeth Rochelle FeelJoy

Does life get better? Continue to the last read.

MORAL

OF

THE

STORY

Chapter 10
Moral of the story

When I think back to the impossible situations that God has delivered me from, I'm calm not panicked. I still have bills and even student loans to pay off, but with programs such as Fed Loan Servicing, I qualify for forbearance, after 20 years and I still can't pay, my student loan debt is forgiven. I would only have to pay taxes on what was forgiven. I'm working hard actively looking for better employment so it won't come to that, but it's a pleasant assurance to have if it does.

According to Sex and the City (2002, S4 E17) there is a line that goes:

"It's tempting to wish for the perfect boss, or the perfect parent, or the perfect outfit, but maybe the best any of us can do is not quit; play the hand we've been given and accessorize the outfit we've got." Yes, I quit the job and is taking a break on life, but according to an appeal I filed with my job, I quit for good cause, any other reasonable human being could not have continued working under those conditions. To avoid being burnt out on life itself, I thought it best to take a break. I have; however, accessorized my life by managing my current situations instead of running from it. When I lost my job at the news station, followed by the work-from-home permanent one, I stayed. Even while faced with a law suit against Meineke and lost, even while faced with massive debt, and all while abandon

Moral of the story

by ex-lovers and family, I stayed in Tara. While the experience of staying put is new for me, the benefits of overcoming my obstacles hold a more satisfying reward. In my apartment I made an office, and hanging on the wall of my office is a beautiful picture with the words: BLOOM WHERE YOU ARE PLANTED. For some strange reason God has planted me here in Tara, Tennessee. No matter where I ran I always found my way back.

It has been 2 years since I have state hopped. I am still living in the apartment that is income base and now fully furnished. It is a comfort to know that money will not dictate rather or not I have a roof over my head. It is a comfort that I am still getting use to and am grateful for. I have also set boundaries for myself that I dare not cross; such as, my life with God. I have kept my promise and stopped smoking cigarettes and having sex, I won't even let a guy kiss me. Because of my promise, I avoided sleeping with men that were wrong for me, and instead got to see them for exactly who they were. I avoided a married man, community penises, and a child molester. As for a royal, at the end of 2017, reports have confirmed that Prince Harry will be married. He's marring a black lady. Although; I was sure it would be to me. He and his fiancée even look alike. At least the fantasy of someday being a royal helped keep my morals intact. Everyday isn't perfect, but I believe God is taking care of me and has been since before I made that promise. My relationship with my family has altered slightly; my stepmother has apologized to me since then, while the relationship with Stepdad is still nonexistent. I tried to have a relationship with my sisters and brothers, but found I was the only one trying, so I just gave up altogether. Pastor Aunt and I are talking to each other again since the car situation, but with a side of caution on my part. Besides; coming from the direction of poverty, it's hard to hold a grudge when everyone is in constant need of something. I am also grateful to her for always opening her doors to me, even if it was for a price. And finally; I want to give a big thank you to this whole experience: To every shelter that took me in and fed me, to every job that took a chance and hired me, to public assistance programs that picked up the bills I could not afford, thank you. Lastly; to every reader of this book: Plan your life and work your plan so that this won't be your story.

I wrote this book as a way to go back in time and re-evaluate my life, to see where I went wrong. After 10 years (can't believe it's been that long), I finally put an ending to this journey as a warning to others: Not to make the same mistakes I've made. *Those who can't do teach,* or warn in my case. Currently; I am unemployed and in therapy. I've taken some time off to re-evaluate my circumstances. Since my living arrangements are no longer an issue while in the Housing Program (pay rent according to income), I can channel my energy towards becoming a better me. I want to make this book available to the public, to give a voice to those who have gone through similar circumstances. I do not want sympathy for what I've gone through because it's over with. This experience is in my past.

If there are proceeds to be made from this book I want to give it to charity, from each state that buys, that money will go to that state to distribute to those in need. I'm already blessed with enough charity. It'll make me feel better to give back, sort-of-like those people who have to spend every day or else they'll go mad. By this book going public, I'm hoping to gain recognition in set up on another book I'm writing about: How to prepare for life after graduating high school, all the things I wish I'd done. I want to enlist the help of celebrities like: Rico Rodriguez from the television show-Modern Family. He plays a high school graduate

Moral of the story

transitioning into college and is currently doing so in real life. I; along with many readers, would like to know how he approached the transition. I also want to insert written excerpt from Justin Bieber on how he maintains being rich and who to trust at such a young age. Then; I want an excerpt from the parents of these young celebrities like: Tichina Arnold from the television show- Everybody hates Chris. She has a daughter named- Alijah Kai just entering High school. Lynn and Rick Bynes are the parents of celebrity, Amanda Bynes and I'm curious on their approach in delegating authority. I'm hoping to reach a wide audience, to open their understanding about the other side of gaining an education, and that it involves more preparation rather than just having a degree.

While in High School, take the opportunity to work or intern at places that you want to make into a career. High School is the perfect situation to do so because one should have some sort of security living with your guardians. It's difficult figuring out your next move on top of figuring out where you're going to sleep as you've just read. Plus; businesses prefer working or interning a younger crowd. Somehow younger is always better in the business world. If you're reading this and you're in college, don't freak out. My story maybe an exception to the rule. But now that you've read my story make it your priority to make connections with businesses. Advertise yourself and let businesses know who you are loud and clear. If you're reading this after college and you've felt short changed, then learn from your experiences and help me warn others to plan for their lives. College is not the enemy, but careless decisions could be.

After College When You Don't Have A Plan

COMMENTS

Leave a comment...

Vicky127

I got all the way to the end and this is it!

Miketheman

Vicky127 Omg- right!

Moral of the story

Elizabeth Rochelle FeelJoy

Vicky127 and Miketheman Don't get upset, this is a unique experience in where you get to travel back in time to this relevant story, and read the other side of having a college degree.

Miketheman

Elizabeth Rochelle FeelJoy Not you again! Where is the happy ending? She didn't even win the lottery.

After College When You Don't Have A Plan

BigPaul

Miketheman I know right.

Lacy Hamilton

Miketheman Agree and equally upset!

John1294

Miketheman I believe I'm going to have nightmares about Elizabeth Rochelle FeelJoy's upbeat, happy disposition, to this serious problem.

Moral of the story

Elizabeth Rochelle FeelJoy

Miketheman, BigPaul, Lacy Hamilton, John1294 Sometimes there are no *happy endings*. This is not an American type story; it's the Irish type-The Devil's Own, Wikipedia quote-1997.

Jackie1workaholic

Elizabeth Rochelle FeelJoy What in the-hell-type of a response is that?

Suzanne Merriweather

Elizabeth Rochelle FeelJoy *"Sometimes there are no happy endings."* True, but toss me a bone.

REFERENCES

References

Montañez, R. (2013). A Boy, A Burrito, And A Cookie. Mustang, OK: Tate.

Campbell, E and Campbell, T. (2012). Go Get It [Mary Mary]. Greatest Hits. United States: Columbia.

Hunte, A and Sewell-Ulepic, J. (2009). Empire state of mind [Alicia Keys and Robin Jay Z]. The Blueprint 3. United States: Roc The Mic Studios.

King, M. P, and Star, D. and Parker, S. J, and Melfi, J. P. (2002). A Vogue Idea. Sex and the City. United States: HBO.

House of Names. (2000-2017). Payne Surname, Family Crest & Coats of Arms. https://www.houseofnames.com/payne-family-crest.

Wikipedia. (2017, November 9). Supplemental Nutrient Program. https://en.wikipedia.org/wiki/Supplemental_Nutrition_Assistance_Program.

Police Break Into Home, Evict Mother And Week-Old Son. Julian Hattem – https://www.huffingtonpost.com/2009/12/01/police-break-into-home-ev_n_375795.html.

September 15 Birthday Astrology. Jill M. Phillips - https://entertainment.howstuffworks.com/horoscopes-astrology/september-15-birthday-astrology.html.

Riley, T and Thicke, R. (2010). It's in the Mornin [Snoop Dogg and Robin Thicke]. Sex Therapy. United States: Interscope.